ANDREW CRUICKSHANK
An Autobiography

WEIDENFELD AND NICOLSON
London

For Curigwen

Contents

Illustration Acknowledgements

The photographs in this book are reproduced by kind permission of:

Peter Adamson 14 above; BBC Hulton Picture Library 3 above, 11 above, 12 below; Nobby Clark 15 above and below left; Chris Davies 14 below; John Haynes 16 above; Mander & Mitchenson 4 above, 5 above, 7; Angus McBean 4 below (courtesy of H. M. Tennent), 6; Photo Source/Keystone Collection 10 below right, 13 above; Robert Pitt 8, 9 below left, 10 below left; David Sim 9 below right (courtesy of H. M. Tennent Ltd); Sport & General Press Agency 9 above, 12 above, 13 below; Weidenfeld & Nicolson Archives 16 below (photographer Arabella Ashley); Alex 'Tug' Wilson 15 below right.

Preface

A letter to my grandchildren

An actor who knows something of his craft may be expected, when he attempts to give expression to his life, to begin at the beginning. That I have not done so calls for an apology to my grandchildren who it seems are avid to know something of my childhood, though I would point out to them that flickers from my youth surface in the text, as they frequently do, uninvited, in my mind.

With this apology there must go an explanation of the theory on which I base my life. Few really appreciate the full implications of the explosion at Hiroshima in 1945. The devastation was appalling we know. What we were reminded of in the most dramatic way is that the world is in continual motion. While everything moves from the planets to the minutest particle, there is paradoxically a universal awareness that we occupy One World.

It was absurd that an actor should feel he could do anything about this. Hiroshima was the result of a great scientific insight into the nature of reality made manifest by a political act to create a completely new weapon of war. The issues involved remained in the hands of politicians.

While brooding on Einstein's theories, I came upon an earlier scientific theory at which the imagination of the artist boiled over. It is *this* theory that underlies my book.

Some decades before Einstein produced his general theory of relativity in 1905, an Austrian called Boltzmann suggested that there was a natural tendency of any state of order to turn of its own accord into a less orderly state, but not *vice-versa*. This very simple insight is the ground for the scientist's view of the unidirectional flow of the time from past to future.

But of all artists the actor in his craft is always in the present moment, the now of the experience. Indeed, I saw at the time, just before 1950, that all art was created by a civilized society to defy this disorderly movement of nature. I saw that I was engaged in the folly of persuading everyone that they were artists who could thus transcend nature. This was not a political or academic doctrine. It could only be demonstrated in life. Accept this book, therefore, my grandchildren, with my apologies that it is not perhaps what you expected. At the risk of making a fool of myself I have tried to throw some light on that small corner of the world's activity which we know as the theatre.

AC

Prologue

I was born on Christmas Day, 1907, in Aberdeen, and am therefore a Scotsman. John Buchan says that every Scotsman is born a metaphysician. All I know is that I am not an Englishman.

It was evening; the night was quiet. There was only myself in the operations room on the first floor and downstairs the sergeant clerk waiting for any messages that might arrive. It was July 1944 and I was the duty officer at the army headquarters in South Wales.

I had volunteered into the Royal Welch Fusiliers while playing at the Old Vic in *The Tempest* during the late summer of 1940. Only when I started my recruit training later that year did I realize that I was too old to be loved by the army, which has a continual flirtation with youth that can be dispatched to eternity with messages of love and forgetfulness.

I had acted my way with some ease through the various stages of my training and now found myself in Abergavenny, the army having taken over most of South Wales to train real troops and provide safety areas for the artillery of General George Patton's US Third Army.

This evening was no night before Agincourt. Operation Overlord, the invasion of Normandy, had just been launched. I was waiting impatiently for the BBC to start broadcasting Ibsen's *Peer Gynt*, directed by Tyrone Guthrie, with Ralph Richardson as Peer.

I had spent four years at the Old Vic, from 1937 to 1940, and two names from all that period stand out in my mind: Tyrone Guthrie and Harley Granville-Barker. They had directed productions of the two pinnacles of Shakespeare's achievement, *Hamlet* and *King Lear*, in both of which I had appeared.

Guthrie's *Peer Gynt* now began to come across the airwaves. When I first came to London at the end of 1928, I saw a production of *The Wild Duck* at the Everyman Theatre, Hampstead, and now the same feelings poured over me. Ibsen communicates the matter of his plays in a unique way. Some scientists say that the magical number is two. So it is: waves and particles, protein and acid, men and women. With Ibsen, it is illusion and reality. Peer, a farmer of a rotting state, has a vocation as a poet of dreams and lies. He is engaged in a fantastic search for a self he does not know he possesses. The pattern of the play is ambiguous, in tune with Peer's weird imaginings.

On the radio Richardson had a disembodied voice that conveyed beautifully the continuing uncertainties of Peer's postures. Guthrie had cut the play so that on radio it had a sharper edge than in the theatre.

On that silent wartime night, Peer Gynt seemed to be asking questions of myself.

Was I by way of being a poet? Was an actor's life a compact of dreams and lies? Had I a self behind my vocation?

Ludwig Wittgenstein in his *Philosophical Investigations* says that every inner process must have its outward criteria.

At all events, as much as possible I must bind my inner thoughts with things, facts, so that my imagination must continually be related in some way to concrete reality. Unlike Peer, I had a self which I must define. At first sight my vocation as an actor wasn't a help since most people after Plato have regarded it as a dispensable profession. One thing was clear: *my vocation was the most serious thing in the world to me.*

I suppose I meant that, through my profession, I would discover an identity for myself that would give a coherence to the diversity of my experiences. An actor is in a privileged position. He can use his public *persona* as a sort of pseudonym to protect his private life. At the same time, he can regard his vocation as a participation in the most profound kind of reality.

My wife, Curigwen, was with child. In 1945, while we were still in Abergavenny, Harriet was born on 15 July at the Cottage Hospital. Our doctor, Dr Parry, an ardent golfer, was summoned from the ninth tee and, after delivery, rejoined his partners on the fourteenth green.

1 Farewell to 'the Flash'

Few actors can have been demobilized from the army on a Friday, and begun rehearsing the following Monday. Emlyn Williams had written to me saying he had rewritten *Spring 1600*, a half-success of his of the mid-thirties, and wanted me to play Richard Burbage in it. The play dealt with the building of the Globe Theatre and the first performance there of *Twelfth Night*.

The play was to be presented at the Lyric Theatre, Hammersmith, by the Company of Four: Baxter Somerville (the lessee), Hugh 'Binkie' Beaumont (of H. M. Tennent), Norman Higgins (of The Arts Theatre, Cambridge) and Rudolph Bing, looking for somewhere to set up an international festival of the arts. The aim of the company was to produce new work, and, at least for this first play, to cast it mainly from people who had been in the Forces.

In spite of the successful ending of the war, there was a great deal of uncertainty and movement. Our small family, Marty, Harriet, Curigwen and I moved to London to a temporary refuge with Curigwen's brother in the vicarage of St Peter's, Eaton Square, where Ivor was an assistant priest. By this time he had given me Kierkegaard's *Either-Or*. I found it immediately accessible and it has had a profound effect upon my life.

It was round this time that the BBC initiated the Reith Lectures with Robert Oppenheimer, the leader of the Manhattan Project which had produced the atom bomb. The Lectures provided a glimpse of the new world that the devastation of Hiroshima had revealed. He used a sentence which has a special place in my memory: 'If you tell me where an atom is, I cannot tell you its speed; if you tell me its speed, I cannot tell you where it is.'

This was the new kind of equation we had to solve, to live with. The nature of time and light was to become my main preoccupation over the next few years. An actor is always aware of time as he inflects the pulse of a sentence and automatically adjusts the weight of his response to the demands of the playwright.

Great plays emerge in periods of a special kind of certainty, and as far as I could see we had passed such a moment. In the late twenties, when I began acting, the organization of my profession was divided between a few and decreasing number of actor-managers whose main audiences were schools studying their obligatory Shakespeare play, and commercial companies, touring the latest West End success. *Journey's End* had six companies touring at one time, such was the abundance of theatre that had sprawled over the country in the nineteenth and early twentieth centuries. They were mostly Royals of some kind, occasionally an Empire, frequently a Palace.

However, anything that reflected the golden age of the nineteenth century had been punctured by the Second World War and was stumbling about trying to make sense of the new discoveries that were exploding in every direction. Sometimes a classical gleam could be detected, a Lyceum would sprout, suggesting a familiarity with Aristotle, and there was the Academy, a cinema where before the War I could see on film my two favourite actors, Louis Jouvet and Michel Simon.

Spring 1600 was something of a success. There was a sense in which the building of the Globe was a new era and now we too were on the verge of beginning a new era. It prompted the producer to take it on a short tour in the hope that it might come in to the West End if a theatre were available. Alas, none was, but it gave me time to measure the new situation of the theatre and the country.

Politically, the Labour Party expressed the country's new demands in health, housing and so on, but there could also be sensed an uncertainty, and a recognition that the problem of coming to terms with the new world would not be solved by a retreat into insularity. Even before the war, our insularity had not cloaked our nakedness.

I remembered the First World War vividly: my mother, in Scotland, working in a munitions factory; a cup of tea and a bun for my dinner; the pain and euphoria of the first Armistice Day. And as the years passed there remained the pain and poverty, always the poverty. The rooms with no linoleum and, outside the strikes and then the depression of the late twenties which forced my father to leave Aberdeen.

Then in 1933 there arrived on the international scene Roosevelt in America, and Hitler in Germany; Mussolini had already arrived, but was not yet in the top league. I believed that Britain had cut herself off from her roots, from Europe.

Alec Guinness was playing in Sartre's *Huis Clos* (*Vicious Circle*) at a club theatre about the same time that the Company of Four introduced Sartre's work at the Lyric, Hammersmith. Sartre is not a great dramatist, but he had an originality that was sadly missing in British theatre at this time. Not even Shaw could have written a play about Communism like *Les Mains Sales* (*Crime Passionel*).

When *Spring 1600* ended I was sent a prophetic play by Vivian Connell: *The Nineteenth Hole of Europe*. It portrayed nobility of a kind in a Europe decayed and abused. While I was playing in this at the Granville, Waltham Green (later a film studio), Fabia Drake had seen me, and when she came to direct Robert Donat in *Much Ado About Nothing*, she asked me to play Claudio, Hero's lover.

Few people realize the material nature of the acting profession. They cannot understand why an actor is unable to predict what his year's salary will be, or where he himself might be a month hence. This uncertainty has increased enormously with the new channels of communication: film, radio and television.

The two years before I went to the Memorial Theatre at Stratford in 1950 were at once frustrating and illuminating, with one concrete event that brought me some stability. In 1948 our son, John, was born. With Marty and Harriet, our family was now balanced and complete. Curigwen was astonishing; she was over forty and within five years had produced our family. When the Danish philosopher Søren Kierkegaard went to Berlin in 1838 to escape the stigma of his jilting of Regine Olsen, the freedom he experienced led to profound self-analysis. Now that his work preoccupied me so much, I found myself embarking on a similar process but sustained by a family.

I had plenty of work that had not much purpose.

Donat's short season at the Opera House, Manchester, *Much Ado* and *Bolivar* by Peter Ustinov, was a prelude to London. I had played with Donat before at a prewar Buxton Festival in Goldsmith's *The Good Natured Man* when he had given a wonderfully comic performance. He was really too heavy for Benedick; unlike Gielgud in the same part at Stratford, he had no rapier in his weaponry. But as a comic, he was superb.

Halfway through the first week, having supper in my digs, my inside went mad, and every corner of it was pierced with pain. I shouted for my landlady, who took me to my bed and gave me some brandy (the worst thing, as it happened), but I still shouted 'Get a doctor!' It was twelve at night. The poor woman was terrified. By the time a doctor

3

came, the pain was shooting up my right arm, and to get relief I hung it over the rail at the top of my bed.

I was transported to Withington Hospital, where I was operated on for a perforated duodenum at three in the morning, having signed, in torture, a certificate allowing anaesthetics. The surgeon was Viennese, delightful and urbane. My pain was relieved, Curigwen had been frightened out of her wits but endured, and Patrick Troughton succeeded me in *Much Ado*.

It was while I was recuperating that I made one of the great mistakes of my life. Tyrone Guthrie sent me Robert Kemp's adaptation of Sir David Lindsay's *The Thrie Estaites* (1540), inviting me to choose the part I'd like to play. Much to my dismay, I found the Scots language intractable, and regretfully had to decline. Rudolph Bing had, after much searching, found Edinburgh sympathetic to his idea of an international festival, which opened in 1947. Lindsay's play was to be performed in the Church of Scotland Assembly Hall in 1948; it was a great success. I had forgotten Guthrie's brilliant way with crowds and movement and comic business.

However, Benthall wanted me for Webster's *The White Devil* with Margaret Rawlings, Robert Helpmann and Hugh Griffith. Beginning in Shakespeare, my mind had intuitively adjusted itself to his measure of language. Indeed, since then, a concern with language became central to my work. There is a pulse in a playwright's dialogue which comes from his either having started as an actor, or listened with an actor's mind to how people speak.

I found Webster's language too tortured and equivocal for my pleasure; it fell uneasily on my tongue. While it no doubt suited the devious contortions of Jacobean plotting, my mind was not fastidious enough really to enjoy it.

It was with some relief that after the run of the Webster play the BBC asked me to play Claudius. John Gielgud, of course, was to play Hamlet, Celia Johnson, Ophelia, and it was to be the full version.

2 Guthrie and Barker

I was momentarily out of tune, a condition actors usually experience when they're out of work. But it was not so with me. My brother-in-law, Ivor, had departed to be sub-dean of Jerusalem Cathedral, just in time to catch the Israeli–Arab conflict. We were now on our own, and had moved out of the vicarage, but to just the other side of Chester Square, very happily.

The disharmony was with myself; I was not coordinating what I was now calling to myself the sensibilities of my mind. Coleridge defines the mind's experience as having a primary and a secondary imagination. The actor's imagination is immediate and objective. But there is a secondary imagination which can bring memory into coherence with the mind, and so achieve wholeness. What was the origin of the disturbance?

My mind was disturbed by the idea of playing Claudius again, even on the radio. I believed that since Shakespeare's day his plays had never been performed at the pace he desired. 'Trippingly' is the word Hamlet uses when he advises the Players how to speak his speeches.

The gap in theatrical history made by Cromwell and the English Puritan Revolution and the energy wasted on ecclesiastical irrelevancies reaching a peak in the eighteenth century combined to obscure Shakespeare's original dramatic insights. This was an old story, certainly as old as Socrates, where in fifth-century Athens he had disagreed with Plato over the virtue of the Athenian playwrights in the matter of reality. The bugbear was that plays entertained. To the audience that was their main function, and the players could measure the success of their efforts by the silence or laughter their performances evoked.

5

But to the playwright the notion that his play might entertain was not the main concern when the work itself might have taken months to write, involving decisions over a wide range of life and experience.

Even when I began in the Baynton company in 1929, the stage manager would start the first rehearsal of a new production with the words, 'Now here are the cuts'. The evolution of acting in the nineteenth century had made it unthinkable that any Shakespearean play could be produced in its entirety. If it were, there would be no room for these thoughtful pauses, the self-indulgence of the actor with the voice. There was the underlying feeling that if the plays were taken at speed the audience would not understand them.

But in the early days of our century a new concern about the plays was emerging with the works of Shaw and Granville-Barker in the theatre, Bradley and Dover Wilson among the academics. What was missing was the performance itself.

I don't think Gielgud realized how revolutionary he was being by his new approach to Shakespeare summed up in two directions that I have heard him make 'Think on the lines' and 'No daylight between speeches'. St John Ervine in his life of Henry Irving tells the story of the great actor asking Desdemona in the process of smothering her what were they having for supper that night; a query made possible by excessively elongating the beat of verse.

While Gielgud's phrasing and grace of diction were always exemplary it was the underlying pace of the delivery that ushered in a new way of acting Shakespeare's plays. With Gielgud's speed of delivery, a full production of *Hamlet* in its entirety was now conceivable.

Guthrie was no actor, but as a director he had a passion for pace at the appropriate time. In comedy, which was his true field, he could direct Ruth Gordon in *The Country Wife* to wriggle through five minutes of hilarious contortions in the celebrated letter-writing scene. But with tragedy he had been less certain. *The Cherry Orchard*, yes, but until his full-length production of *Hamlet* with Olivier (1937) and Alec Guinness (1938, in modern dress), Guthrie had never really exposed himself to tragedy.

He was a man of extraordinary complexity: a restless, brilliant mind always retarded, I felt, by a sensitivity over his elongated, gangling body. Always sceptical but never quite careful enough to avoid cynicism. He was a reductionist, and a brilliant inventor of theatre business. He had done a beautiful production of *Love's Labour's Lost*, after which I thought that he had gone over the Shakespeare canon in his mind, and decided that the only tragedy that he wanted to do when the time was ripe was *Hamlet*. Later he was to botch *Othello*.

6

I first really saw him in 1937 at the dress rehearsal of *Macbeth* with Laurence Olivier and Judith Anderson; Michel Saint-Denis was directing, Motley did the scenery, and Darius Milhaud the music. I was playing Banquo.

Scenery at the Old Vic until the Gielgud/Guthrie era had been pretty rudimentary, but with the arrival of designers like Motley, Oliver Messel, and Roger Furse, scenery became more elaborate and the actor's surroundings with the help of the flies had a disconcerting habit of taking off. So it was now in *Macbeth*; on the right of the stage there was a huge tree whose great trunk was supposed to open with the help of the flymen and reveal the witches. Alas, there was much trouble in getting the trunk to yawn.

There was also trouble in the orchestra pit where Herbert Menges was coping with Milhaud's music. Ordinarily, composers have a habit of repeating their tunes to make sure that you've not missed anything the first time. This is fine for the concert hall, but not so good in the theatre. I don't think Milhaud realized the difference and would repeat his tunes which should have been cut; Saint-Denis had too much respect to do this, since Milhaud was after all one of Les Six – which meant that on occasion the tunes sounded like ragtime.

It was nearing midnight, and Duncan was nowhere near Macbeth's 'pleasant seat', nor did it seem likely that he would arrive in the foreseeable future. Something had to be done. Guthrie was summoned from the Queen's Theatre, where he was rehearsing *The School for Scandal* with Gielgud. He stood near me at the back of the stalls, the usual handkerchief tied round his neck. For about five minutes he watched the stage hands struggling with ropes and branches, listened to the piping sounds coming from the pit. Then in the stentorian tone he always adopted when directing he shouted 'Stop!' Then with his arms waving over his head, another familiar gesture, he strode down to the stage.

The play was postponed for two days. Miss Baylis, who was ill in bed, died. Some said at the deep disappointment at the first postponement of a play at her theatre, the Old Vic. I didn't believe it. She was tougher than that, she was also of Sadler's Wells.

In spite of its idiosyncrasies – my head was heightened by a scalp with flowing black hair, something between a Viking who'd forgotten his helmet and a follower of Genghis Khan – the production was something of a success, and Albery transferred it to the New for a short season.

After a short time in Guthrie's gloriously romantic *Midsummer Night's Dream* at the Old Vic with Messel's scenery, Mendelssohn's music,

7

Vivien Leigh and Helpmann, I moved to the top of the hill that overlooks London on which sits Alexandra Palace, the home of prewar television. I had been appearing on television at odd moments since 1937.

I was playing Dr Knox in James Bridie's *The Anatomist*, to be broadcast live on a Sunday and the following Thursday afternoon. I had seen Henry Ainley playing it at the Westminster, and now I began to be aware that, at the age of thirty-one, directors viewed me as beyond juvenilia. My apprenticeship was over. I could begin acting like a French actor, like those I had seen at the Academy cinema; their names rolled off my tongue like the list of English dead: Louis Jouvet, Jules Berry, Pierre Brasseur, Fernandel, Michel Simon. Was this the auld alliance peeping through? I certainly felt a special empathy with the French.

About the same time that I received the letter from Emlyn Williams asking me to play in *Spring 1600*, James Bridie had asked me to join him and Matthew Forsyth at the foundation of the Citizens' Theatre in Glasgow, but we had been away from London for five years and I felt it would not be fair on Curigwen and I declined. Bridie expressed his regret with great grace and later I made a kind of amends by televising two of his plays, *Dr Angelus* and *Meeting at Night* – the latter being the first play that James MacTaggart directed.

In the spring of 1938 I was asked to return to the Old Vic to play Claudius in *Hamlet*, with Guthrie directing. The production was to be the centrepiece of the first Buxton Festival, return to the Old Vic, then embark on a short tour of some Mediterranean countries, sponsored by the British Council as a riposte to the blasts of propaganda by Hitler and Mussolini.

By the time of rehearsal I had learned the part, so there was not that tension during the production period that creates uneasiness. The weather was wonderful. After rehearsals I would walk over Waterloo Bridge, have a meal at Rule's, and as often as I could, take myself to Covent Garden where de Basil's Ballet Russes de Monte Carlo was maintaining the Diaghilev tradition under Léonide Massine, with Tatiana Lichine and a whole bevy of exquisite new dancers. I have always loved women, but ballet dancers seem to have a mystery all their own. They're never fat. The music, too. Symphonies of Berlioz and Brahms being transformed into marvellous movement.

This was the background to my first musings about Shakespeare, the dramatist, and the play I was rehearsing. Apart from O. B. Clarence

(Polonius), Malcolm Keen (the Ghost), and a grizzled, almost deaf Scots actor, Craighall Sherry (the Player King), the cast was very young. Alec Guinness was twenty-six, I was thirty-one, the oldest of a group of actors which also included Anthony Quayle and André Morell. This was what Guthrie wanted: no stars, young people with energy to hold his vision of the play to the end. He wanted actors who could wear the modern dress with grace and move with the rapidity the play demanded so that the four great soliloquies could appear as potent moments of inward silence suddenly made articulate.

Guthrie was extraordinary. The play was having in rehearsals a strange affect on him. It was as though all he had dreamt about producing the play was coming right, and he couldn't believe it. No 'business'; that was what struck me. His fame as an inventor of comic business was legendary, but now there was to be nothing. The play was speaking, and he was letting it speak without distraction. There are actors with a gift for stage business, that is the manipulation of things inspired by a text, to embroider it. Any invention I possessed lay in the use of my voice.

As I remember, only in the spotlights flashing round the theatre after the play scene and the umbrellas in the graveyard scene did he emphasize a situation. No short skirts, no telephones, no smoking, no cocktails. The severity of the men's dress, the grace of the women's, was surrounded by Roger Furse's apt scenery, always beautifully lit by Guthrie, who was a master of his craft.

There were unexpected bonuses to Guthrie's approach. The first production of the play was in the costume of the day. Again, in the eighteenth century the dress was contemporary; producers in the nineteenth century had run riot with elaborate costumes and scenery. The result had been a slowing of delivery in harmony with the under-lying dramatic tone of the century, that is, melodrama.

Now, uncluttered by period costume and trinkets, the actors were free to express an unusual intensity and, because of this, explore a greater variation of colour in the text. But from my point of view I realized truly for the first time the linear, pure quality of the play.

That Shakespeare was an actor is one of the fundamental facts that the English cannot accept. An actor stands in the wings peering at the astonishing thing that is happening on the stage.

Whatever we might think of Hamlet's person, and academics have countless views about this, my feeling is that Shakespeare's familiarity with the original of Hamlet was of such a nature that he was determined to write a play about this one person, and only this one person. I feel that in some way in the middle of his turbulent new world, he saw the

Renaissance fading before him and *Hamlet* was his tribute to it.

I do not think Hamlet is a self-portrait, but it is about a man who, observing the corruption about him, the cruelty of man and nature, could see himself whole and assert simply, 'The readiness is all.'

Listening to Guinness, I brooded on Shakespeare's attitude to the form of the play. I constantly returned to the linear nature of the play. There are moments of turbulence in the part, but always there is a tenderness. In most of his plays there is usually, as in *King Lear*, a balancing counterplot. But not in Hamlet. It is impossible to inflate the revolt over the succession into anything but an excuse for Claudius's plotting.

One day I realized why Guthrie's linear production was so good. The play divides into three parts: what happens to Hamlet when he is in Denmark, what happens in Denmark when Hamlet is in England, what happens to Hamlet when he returns to Denmark. If the three parts were of equal length then Hamlet might not have been the pivot of the play. Harley Granville-Barker notices this and suggests in his *Preface* that Hamlet's visit to England was long enough; anything longer and Claudius might have usurped the stage, which it was in his character to do.

The solution was entirely technical. The first part must be so long as to squeeze the other two parts almost indecently together, and in order to do this Shakespeare gave Hamlet not one soliloquy in which to analyse himself, but four. Round these he could muster enough action to maintain the linear quality of the play, and with it the unique centrality of Hamlet. With *King Lear* he had a very different problem to solve.

Guthrie's production was well received by those not slaves to tradition. But there were those who felt that sending the Old Vic abroad in 1939, especially to Italy, with a modern dress production of their national poet's greatest play would merely confirm something Mussolini had been preaching since we had used sanctions against him in the war with Abyssinia, that the English were decadent. Lord Lloyd, chairman of the British Council, came to see it one night, and gave it his blessing. He only saw one act, but it was clearly enough. The tour went ahead.

Curigwen Lewis was in the touring company. I had not seen her since the previous year, then as a minor member of the company, I had observed her crucifixion as Desdemona between the Othello and Iago of Ralph Richardson and Laurence Olivier with Guthrie uneasily presiding.

We were married on 12 August 1939 in Evancoyd parish church; Radnorshire by her brother, the vicar.

10

'Cruickshank, *King Lear* is a play about antinomies. It's about good and evil, right and wrong, mental pain and physical pain. As Cornwall you're the epitome of evil; there is no redemption in you, and I shall produce your scene with Gloucester so that people will feel it where such evil affects people most, in their stomachs,' Granville-Barker informed me.

And he did. I have always been a sensual actor, and the sensuality of Cornwall's evil was something to exploit, especially when directed so superbly. Cornwall, wounded on his knees, intent at Regan's command to remove Gloucester's other eye, crawls slowly towards the bound Gloucester on his stool, arm outstretched, the thumb of the right hand erect and threatening, slowly (the man is mortally wounded and desperate to perform his last heinous task), slowly, then the stretch towards Gloucester's head, the quick twitch, and Gloucester's scream. Of course, people were sick. There was scarcely a night when I was not told of vomit in the Old Vic bar.

It was Barker's vision, and Barker who contrived this little holocaust. Guthrie could never have talked like that, though he might have invented the scene.

In the spring of 1940, during the phoney war, Gielgud had the audacious idea of opening the Old Vic for a season of two plays, *King Lear* and *The Tempest*, the first to be directed by Barker, the second by George Devine and Marius Goring. He would get a company of stars (I was not of the constellation), mainly his old friends, for this (I believe) his first attempt at the part.

Barker, when invited, at first refused but said that if Lewis Casson visited him in Paris he would pass on his ideas about the play.

For almost three weeks we struggled with what Casson thought Barker's ideas were. Then a fortnight or so before the first night Barker himself arrived, and after seeing the first act of a rehearsal decided to stay and make what he could of Casson's well-meaning tangle. For ten days we worked morning, noon and night. So exciting was the atmosphere that many of the cast would come back to Curigwen's flat in the Adelphi to savour the experience.

I could understand Shaw's dismay when, during the First World War, Barker decided to remove himself from the commercial theatre. The point is that there was no one in England with Barker's rich experience as actor, writer and director – a director of an unusual kind who could combine a familiarity with the new theatre Ibsen's influence was creating, the new naturalistic direction that André Antoine in Paris had been taking, together with a highly enlightened academic's insights into the structure of what was arguably the most profound play ever written.

11

And now, he was in the theatrical presence of the greatest of them all. It was a challenge he couldn't resist. No wonder he took off his jacket to work instead of going to the Athenaeum Club for lunch.

What Barker was saying to me about *King Lear* was that the play is a mosaic, that at its heart the magical number two always occurs. Hamlet appears almost immediately and then is scarcely off the stage until his departure for England; *Lear* opens with the lesser of the two central characters, Gloucester, and his bastard son, Edmund, then Lear makes his entrance; that is the proper order which Shakespeare maintains with wonderful control; in matters spiritual, physical pain rates lower than mental pain; until the two come together on a bench towards the end of the play.

Lear must begin high so that his physical slighting matches his increasing moral awareness as he descends. The children of the two families, Gloucester's sons and Lear's daughters, must approach from opposite sides of the stage so that the structure of the play can be preserved from the mess that the density of its mosaic invites.

These were the opposing lines that Casson couldn't quite grasp. Indeed, what with Guthrie's linear *Hamlet* and Barker's mosaic *King Lear*, I felt the value judgements that we usually feel about plays ('How beautifully you sat down on that chair in the second act!') must yield to a more fundamental kind of judgement, almost mathematical, for only then could we be rid of that self-indulgence which is the bane of English acting and audiences.

I dislike critics who comment on particular bits of business or sounds in a play that have pleased them. In my first company there were actors who never stopped telling me how Irving pulled on his boot in *The Bells*. But, hoist with my own irreverence, there was one exchange between Gielgud and Barker that has stayed with me all my life, and coloured it.

Quite early in the play Lear is affronted by Goneril and in fury curses her, 'Hear, Nature, hear; dear goddess, hear!' Gielgud spoke the line with some pressure, but Barker interrupted him. 'No, no, dear boy,' then almost whispering, 'Hear, Nature, hear; dear goddess, hear!' 'I can't,' said Gielgud. 'But you must,' said Barker. 'If you do not play it like that now, what will happen when . . .' I did not catch what he said precisely but he was clearly indicating the vocal climaxes to the end of the play. It was a lesson in measuring the energy in acting a play.

A lieder singer hears in his mind the last note before he begins. An actor feels he can solve any problem emotionally. But Lear is vast, and requires measure. Knowing the play well I could measure the peaks. Barker's *Preface* to the play was written in 1927; it was now 1940. It was clear he had in between been brooding on the play, but then I know no actor who, having played in *Lear*, is not haunted by it.

The Tempest followed *Lear*, and very soon in a horrible empathy the tempest broke out in France, and all reason departed, and with it the audiences drained away from the theatre. The weather had an obstinate beauty that seemed determined to retain its impartiality. There was a place called Dunkirk and small boats were ferrying a retreating, defeated army home.

I told Curigwen I could bear it no longer, and went up to the Seven Sisters Road to volunteer into the Royal Welch Fusiliers. At the theatre that night I told Jack Hawkins and André Morell what I'd done. They cursed me – and volunteered soon after.

3 Up to Stratford, 1950

After the radio version of the complete *Hamlet*, I was engaged in some quite unmemorable television work when I was invited to go to Stratford in 1949 to join Guthrie. Once again I had to turn him down. This was becoming ridiculous. Then Peter Ustinov wrote *The Indifferent Shepherd* and, with Norman Marshall directing, I joined the cast, which was led by Gladys Cooper and Francis Lister.

Gladys had been in America during much of the war. Francis, I imagine, had been too old for active service. He was a charming benevolent toper, who covered everything with a disappearing smile. He was an actor with a beautiful light touch.

I first met him in 1934 in America where we were to play together in Gordon Daviot's *Richard of Bordeaux*. I was waiting at the stage door of the old Empire theatre at the foot of Times Square when he loped in; he always put his feet down as if he was just going to walk on tiptoe. He swayed about for a moment, then turning to me he said, 'Isn't it funny, I can't get the feel of the boat out of my feet.'

The first night of Ustinov's play was pretty nerve-racking. Gladys was an extremely professional woman, who was also very sensitive. She did not know what sort of reception she'd get; after all she had been one of the great between-wars theatre figures, as actress and manager, at the Playhouse Theatre. Ustinov, following Barker's antinomies, had at the centre of his play, two parsons, one gentle and refined, the other athletic, not unlike Shaw's Morell in *Candida*. Gladys was Francis's wife in the play, and for some reason Norman Marshall, who was no great director, had placed me between them.

Gladys was very nervous. When she appeared however she had an enormous reception which, far from allaying any fears she may have had, made them worse. Francis was taking the whimsical element in his part very much to heart and spent the evening in something of a mist. Cues were intermittent – I felt like a tennis umpire, my head moving in slow motion between them. The agony of the first night over, Gladys had an enjoyable season.

Later in the year, I was again invited to Stratford with an alluring prospect before me. I was to play Wolsey, Julius Caesar, Leonato in *Much Ado About Nothing*, and Kent in *Lear*. The casts were superb: Gielgud, Leon Quartermaine, Harry Andrews, Gwen Ffrangcon-Davies, Peggy Ashcroft, Anthony Quayle, and quite the finest group of young players I have ever been with.

During the summer I was going to move out to Chipping Campden where Curigwen and the children were to join me for their summer holidays. I had no car, and John and Peggy had kindly suggested I could go in with them to Stratford, so that between them the plays were covered. During these trips I learned from Gielgud that every morning he read some extracts from Shakespeare. I don't think I know an actor who is so totally of the theatre.

My memories of Stratford then were of a supreme delight; in the middle of which there was only one thorn....

The 1950 season opened with *Measure for Measure* with Gielgud as Angelo, directed by Peter Brook, a great success. In due course *Henry VIII* followed, with Guthrie directing; he was as formidably comic as ever, with George Rose and Michael Bates as two decadent English lords commenting pungently on the social scene, and drilling a dozen soldiers from the local barracks for Elizabeth's baptism at the end of the play. He stood them in a row diagonally across the stage, then told them he'd count out the beats of the music, thirty-two in all, composed by a great friend of his, Cedric Thorpe Davie, from St Andrew's University.

Meanwhile, they'd form figures of eight along the line, always ensuring by the thirty-second beat they had returned to their original places. They repeated this process until they were perfect. Guthrie then told the stage management to give them the poles. With poles in their hands, they repeated the movements. Guthrie then said, 'Now, the flags! Put them on the poles!' When this was accomplished he inserted the soldiers into the crowds surrounding the baptism; the effect with the music was electric and gave a rich impression of spontaneous delight.

Henry VIII is a minor play. It is doubtful if it is entirely Shakespeare, thus qualifying as a fit subject for Guthrie's extravagant imagination, an imagination which at the same time was as acutely aware of the

15

political elements in the play, such as Cranmer's emergence from a bank of clerics to succeed Wolsey, as of the comic.

But where human business was concerned his imagination was voluptuous, difficult to restrain. One day he came up to me and said 'I think Wolsey had gout!' I must have looked at him with some uncertainty for he went on to explain how great a host he was, the legendary parties at Hampton Court, his power; not the full gout but enough to compel me to use a stick to walk.

I felt enormously vulnerable. After all I'd been in what I now regarded as his most masterly production, but had refused two invitations from him. Also there was a sneaking suspicion in my mind that it might just work. Had I been in a film by Buñuel it would, and certainly some of the business in the play had a Gallic absurdity. I did not argue. Any feelings I had that Wolsey was being reduced to a caricature, I smothered.

For an audience at the Academy cinema it would have worked; but it did not for an English audience who always regarded Wolsey as noble, in spite of his deviousness – he had built Hampton Court and founded Cardinal College, Oxford. To see him hobbling to the front of the stage, banished by the king, crippled with gout and yet still hoping to appeal to an audience's sympathy with the lines:

> Had I but served my God with half the zeal
> I served my king, he would not in mine age
> Have left me naked to mine enemies.

was asking too much. In my mind I could hear them muttering, 'Not on your nelly, you had it coming to you'.

The experiment was not a success. After only a few performances I received a note from Guthrie with a kind of apology, telling me to cut the gout.

Some time later I was in the street and heard someone hurrying after me. It was a drama critic whom I had never met, T. C. Worsley. Apparently he'd seen the performance the previous night, and been very moved. I must have looked stupid because he went on, 'It was so different!' Then a pause. 'Jolly good!' I thanked him and walked away. Worsley was very reassuring which was just as well because a little later I was to meet two people of great theatrical importance, Theresa Helburn and Lawrence Langner.

They were visiting Stratford to see the plays and asked to meet me. They introduced themselves as the directors of the New York Theatre Guild, the most important play-producing company in America. They told me that they were reviving Shaw's *St Joan* in 1952 – two years hence – and would like me to play Warwick in it if I were free. I said that free or not, I would do it.

My mind has a habit of instant recollection. (I don't believe I am different in making connections from anyone else but actors have a rich vineyard of memories from which to pluck.) It was spring 1939 with the Old Vic company in Italy. We were in Naples. Lewis Casson, Sybil Thorndike's husband, was in the company, now playing Polonius. Curigwen and I went with him one morning to Pompeii. The ruins are not very extensive, so about midday Lewis suggested that we might share a taxi to climb over the hill to Amalfi. There he knew a monastery that had been converted into a superb hotel where the food was first rate.

So we found ourselves in the converted monastery waiting for lunch. Since Pompeii Lewis had become increasingly agitated, which we put down to his jumpy Welshness. Eventually after one of his absences he returned triumphantly, beaming.

'I've found it,' he said.

Apparently, he had found the bedroom with a legend on the door to witness that he and Sybil had slept in that room in 1924.

Ibsen had stayed in that monastery. So had Mussolini while planning his march on Rome in 1922. But I didn't tell Lewis.

They had gone to Amalfi on their first holiday away from their children with the script of *St Joan*, which they were going to produce in London later that year. It was a famous cast; whenever he could, the critic James Agate would recall it as I found myself doing: Lyall Swete, Eugene Leahy, Lewis Casson, Lawrence Anderson, Ernest Thesiger, playing the principal male parts.

But the irony was that Shaw had let the Theatre Guild have the first production with Winifred Lenihan as Joan, out of gratitude for all they had done for his work in America. Now they were repeating it with Uta Hagen. But that was two years hence.

Rehearsing at Stratford was enormously exciting once I had restored Wolsey to health. And as we were doing *Lear* Barker naturally cropped up. I remember once during the rehearsal of the last scene with Gloucester, Gielgud, standing not far from me in the stalls with his minute copy of the play, squinnying at something he'd written then shouting out, 'Barker told me that I should play this scene as though there was a pain shooting through my head!' Later, when the play had been running some time, Peggy Ashcroft and I were standing in the wings watching this scene. Then at the words 'This a good block', John slowly dipped his head against the head of the blind Gloucester, for all the world as I used to press my head against the cold glass of the window if I had a headache. We both shivered for a moment. The theatre is wonderful when it reveals its depths spontaneously.

There were other things too.

The first Beatrice and Benedick of Gielgud and Ashcroft. With scenery and costumes by Mariano Andreu. Was there ever such elegance?

On the first night of *Julius Caesar*, Quayle, as Antony, and I, as Caesar, passed through the crowd on Caesar's first entrance to descend to the pit below the stage. Gielgud and Andrews, as Cassius and Brutus, were left to carry on with their scene. Cassius's vitriolic passion I had never heard the like of before. 'What's happening?' I said to Quayle. Gielgud had done nothing like this at rehearsal. But then, as he proved subsequently in the film version with Marlon Brando, leaving the main tragedies aside, Cassius is the character in Shakespeare for which Gielgud has all the gifts: the slight frame, the intensity, the sharp movement, the spitting speech.

Before the Stratford season he had appeared in Christopher Fry's *The Lady's Not for Burning* and was contracted to play the piece in New York when Stratford finished. But the season had been so successful it was decided to extend it. There was the question of Angelo in *Measure for Measure* and, importantly for Peter Brook, the succeeding tour of Germany where the play was to be produced in Düsseldorf, Wiesbaden, Hamburg and Berlin. I was asked to replace Gielgud, and Peter Brook was kind enough to entertain me to three breakfasts at the Shakespeare Hotel to make sure I understood his conception of Angelo. I could appreciate his anxiety. We were to appear in Berlin, where we would be under the scrutiny of Brecht's Berliner Ensemble, whom he greatly admired.

The 1950 season was proving phenomenally successful. Perhaps it was the first time since the war had ended that the British people were being reminded of their heritage, reminded impeccably because Quayle was supervising the great richness for which Shakespeare's plays provide excuses: sets, costumes, music, cast combined a feast of beauty.

One evening at the Dirty Duck (officially, the Black Swan) I met Aneurin Bevan and his wife, Jenny Lee, with Michael Foot and his wife, Jill Craigie; they were seeing the plays and had just been punting on the Avon. Bevan asked me what I was going to do next, after the season finished. I told him that we were going to Germany with *Measure for Measure*. He snorted, and roared with laughter, 'Ha, the government's foreign policy having failed, they're sending the actors to sort it out, eh!'

18

Something like this had happened to me before when Lord Lloyd came to the Old Vic to sanction the modern *Hamlet* which had taken everywhere it went by storm. I could not guarantee that the same would happen in Germany with *Measure for Measure*, though it was one of their favourite plays.

A few weeks later the company was embarking at Naples for Alexandria. The neighbouring ship was a 'Strength through Joy' ship with which the Germans were peppering the Mediterranean at the time; we had been almost smothered by German tourists at Pompeii. Towards the evening, the 'Sieg Heil's started, and guns were popping balloons into the air. Reaching a certain height, they burst and flags floated down to the harbour; there were two kinds of flag, the swastika and the Italian flag, but the swastika was always a little bigger.

One thing that the Strength through Joy ship at Naples confirmed: my loathing of crowds. I could repeat with an inner zest Kierkegaard's saying that 'The crowd is untruth'.

My overall impression of Germany in 1950 was of silence – not a dead silence, but a silence with a pulse in it ready to beat. The streets were broken-down but clean, punctuated every now and then by massive pyramids of rubble that the Germans would clear away once they'd broken through the silence. There was no Hiroshima here, nor in France, for that matter, but devastation of an inordinate depth, not only in physical matter, but in spirit as well. The physical side they were beginning to rebuild; it was as though after the Berlin airlift of 1948 their base was now secure and they could begin again – with theatre.

At Düsseldorf, actor/director Gustaf Gründgen's wife, Marianne Hoope, was playing in Maxwell Anderson's *Anne of a Thousand Days*. In Wiesbaden we saw a Lehár operetta done with a style as rich as Oswald Stoll's efforts in our own prewar Coliseum, complete with white wigs, white gloves and glistening chandeliers. In Hamburg I saw opera in a partially improvised opera house, and in Berlin Peter Brook could spend his time at the Berliner Ensemble. The Wall had not yet been built.

This was Germany in hiatus. How would she take off? Hiroshima had forced us all to understand something of science, and I began to use the triangular image of the molecule as a model. So it was that I saw fifth-century Athens and Elizabethan England as molecules of insight, technique and energy. How did Germany measure up to this kind of analysis? Money was necessary, if techniques were to evolve and be paid for. In fifth-century Athens, the winner of the contest for plays was granted a chorus by the state; in England, Shakespeare was

19

financed by Leicester, than as powerful as if he were king himself. Who would finance the technique of recovery here? Why, those mainly responsible for the devastation, the Americans, of course! In all history, the Marshall Plan for Germany, France, Italy and Japan was the greatest act of altruism and had the most profound, unpredictable effects in the political sphere.

Since the war I had been reading a great deal of Kierkegaard. One of the effects of Hiroshima, I thought, was to discredit all systematic thought, in that the world was now so volatile that no system could contain it. It was a state that Kierkegaard had anticipated in his study of uncertainty. He says that a logical system is possible only at the price of disregarding contingencies, the facts of uncertainty.

The two great systems in the Western world that disregard these facts and hold to their own logic are the Communist Party, and the Christian Church, both of which believe that the truth has been once revealed, and cannot move, in a world where everything moves.

It was astonishing to me that, for instance, while West Germany retained its identity, it did not turn to Communism. Before the war there had been strong Communist elements in Munich. Ernst Toller's Expressionist play *Masses and Man* (1921) had been performed in England in 1923 but how could I account for the Christian Democrat Party?

It was too much to attribute it to Kierkegaard. Such overt political work was not in his syllabus. But it was possible, I thought, that his notion of indirect communication was highly relevant to the intelligent German. All the great German theologians and philosophers before the war had been influenced by him: Karl Barth, Dietrich Bonhoeffer, Rudolf Bultmann, Emil Brunner, Paul Tillich, Karl Jaspers, and Martin Heidegger.

There was a great mayor of Cologne, Konrad Adenauer, who was stamping his personality on the Christian Democrat Party, and the Socialist Party was achieving an entity. When the Marshall Aid became available, both parties subscribed to Heideggers's '*dasein*' without really knowing it. It was a concept which not merely suited the situation but contained an openness in harmony with the movement of the times.

Dasein is Heidegger's description for the 'thereness' of life, difficult to understand in the individual, but all too apparent to the German who could see the 'thereness' of his economic world shattered, and now, given the means of finance, could see a way by which he could restore his culture and practise the Greek attribute of thereness, 'nothing too much'. While recognizing the size of the problems he would not allow them to be obfuscated by proliferating organizations.

Given the increasing density of the world, the German and Japanese economies are the models in that sphere by which the rest of the world can steer a course. Marxism with its emphasis on labour has no answer to the new phoenix that has arisen out of Hiroshima.

After three weeks in Germany I returned to England. In that time no one had mentioned the holocaust. I felt that lay beyond economics.

4 America – A Stage on my Way

After a few television plays and much reading, the invitation from the Theatre Guild to go to America in 1951 duly arrived. I had played Warwick in *St Joan* before in an Old Vic tour during the 1940 'phoney war' and the part soon came back to me so that during the period of rehearsal I felt much as I had done during the rehearsals of *Hamlet*, free to indulge in American acting, which was at something of a peak before becoming attenuated by television and the dispersal of film production. I saw my first Tennessee Williams play, *The Rose Tattoo*, with Maureen Stapleton.

I had also been caught up in the current fever of the baseball World Series then being decided in a drawn-out contest between the New York Yankees and the Brooklyn Dodgers, so that any time I was wanted for rehearsal I had to be summoned from the bar next to the Cort Theatre on West 48th Street.

Before the play opened, Lawrence Langner wrote an article for the *New York Times* about his acquaintance with Shaw and the writing of *St Joan*. Apparently Charlotte, Shaw's wife, had decided that he should write a play about St Joan, so that she went to a lot of trouble to place biographies and articles about Joan in Shaw's way and eventually Shaw's imagination was fired.

The play opened successfully, and Uta Hagen was very good. I did a couple of recordings with the Lunts, playing Colonel Pickering to Lynn Fontanne's Eliza and Alfred Lunt's Higgins in *Pygmalion*, and with Fontanne in J. M. Barrie's one-act *The Old Lady Shows her Medals*. I found Lunt very congenial because we both agreed about Shaw's writing for actors. He shares with Shakespeare a marvellous awareness of dramatic speech and what can sit easily on an actor's tongue. To the dramatist, language is always doubled-edged; it must make sense in his dramatic pattern, and it must sit easily with diction.

I had heard Oscar Hammerstein, rehearsing a musical, *Music in the Air*, in the Ziegfeld Theatre, chiding his cast at their slovenly speech with the most beautiful language in the world. I wouldn't go that far, but I was moved to hear him say it.

Then what I had been unconsciously awaiting emerged. Eva le Gallienne came to my dressing room one day; she said she was doing a recording of *Hedda Gabler* in her own translation. Would I like to play Judge Brack? This was my first Ibsen. I said, blithely, of course. Whatever it is that fuels the feelings, mine were now at furnace heat, and as always, memory came romping into mind, Ralph Richardson in *Peer Gynt* on a quiet evening in Abergavenny just before Hiroshima.

I read it once, I read it twice. Then I remembered Jean-Louis Barrault quoting Jouvet on a play he'd been asked to be in, and disliked, 'Could we live with these people?' I asked the same question about the people in *Hedda Gabler* and gave myself the same answer. Would I like to spend a weekend with the Macbeths? Or join Medea in a cocktail?

Yet, reading it a third time, I found the language falling easily on my tongue, always the first test of a play for me, then forming an idea of how I should play the Judge. I was in the extraordinary situation of rehearsing a play whose characters I disliked, yet enjoying doing it. In fact, the situation is not so unusual for the professional actor. He may see a play in the theatre, he may read it, but until he is himself involved in it as an actor the full potential of the structure cannot be gauged. Particularly is this so with great works.

Ibsen's discoveries had released tides of naturalism in every country. After Ibsen, no self-respecting dramatist wrote in verse. Those who did so, like Paul Claudel or T.S. Eliot, did so under a Christian dispensation. Wherever one turned in the European theatre, a new language prevailed. Pirandello, Strindberg, Chekhov, Shaw, Joyce, and in the USA, Eugene O'Neill. What distinguished Ibsen's realism from the naturalism of these others? Had Ibsen alone the audacity or courage to see society as a cesspool, a pool of diseased fish? Why, I asked myself during rehearsal, was I enjoying so much fishing in this murky pool? The play itself did not yield an answer. I had to wait. But my curiosity was whetted. I was still reading Kierkegaard, and both he and Ibsen were Scandinavians. And in my youth in Aberdeen the sky in winter as I looked beyond the coast would glow with the Northern lights.

It was getting towards Christmas. The play had been recorded, though I never heard it. I had experienced New York in its extremities, the heat of the summer scarcely endurable, and the snow of the winter, so much of it; in between, one of the beauties of the world, the fall in New England. But I had now other things on my mind.

Before 1952 arrived there was Hogmanay, the last day of the old year. Brooks Atkinson, the drama critic of the *New York Times*, knowing I was a Scotsman, invited me to a party. It was very thoughtful of him. At his party we fell to talking about presents that people had received. I said that last year my wife had given me all dozen volumes of C. K. Scott Moncrieff's translation of Proust's *Remembrance of Things Past*. At which one young man said he'd read it crossing the Atlantic. I looked at him incredulously, and murmured, facetiously, 'In a plane, I presume?' It was time to go.

It was 1952, a new year. A couple of months and I'd be on my way home. I realized that I was buoyant. Not that buoyancy assured by good spirits, though these were not in short supply; no, I mean I was in one of those periods where the imagination hovers over the mind and toys with the abundance of prospects before it. My mind has always responded to the mosaic; in my quieter moments of reflection I have always realized that the most an actor can achieve is a vivid synthesis.

Until the twentieth century the English theatre was dominated by Shakespeare, old English comedy, some farce and pantomime. One fell into the hierarchical pattern of the structure, and if gifts were revealed then a line of parts could be occupied in that structure, as one moved from company to company like a commercial traveller showing off his particular wares.

The short episode of Ibsen made me realize that the century until Hiroshima had been gradually dismantling the structure in all its places; in the words of Shakespeare's Ulysses, degree was being taken away, and if discord was not following, a great uncertainty was permeating the oddments.

The market for the actor was still large, partly because the classical structures were being replaced by new fields that required his expertness. But a new measure was being danced, and I had to learn the new movement and steps. We lasted a couple of months into the new year, then the play finished. I had been friendly during the run with an English actor, Frederic Worlock, who had been settled in the States for years; we would share a communion at St Thomas' Episcopal Church in Fifth Avenue. Before I left for home, he presented me with a large volume, celebrating the First Twenty-Five Years of the *New Yorker*. I think it's probably the most fruitful gift I have ever received. If my children have any wit at all, it's because they've been brought up on James Thurber, Ogden Nash and their like. Almost the last thing I heard in New York was of the death of King George VI. The possibilities for a new mosaic, a new synthesis were enormous.

Some time before I arrived back in London, a new thriller by Frederick Knott, *Dial M for Murder*, had been seen on television. I had scarcely arrived home when I was asked to go and see John Fernald at the Westminster Theatre. He invited me to play Detective Inspector Hubbard. Because the play had been done on television, it was the myth of the time that everyone had seen it; and consequently there would be no audience in the theatre for it.

The play had been bought by James Sherwood, not an acknowledged management, but a passionate lover of the theatre from Leeds who'd sold his business, and wanted to enjoy his freedom. Thane Parker, the shrewd manager of the Westminster Theatre, persuaded Sherwood that his theatre was the ideal green for him to bowl on. (Everyone in the theatre knows that the Westminster is a most difficult house to run.)

Raymond Huntley, who had played Hubbard on television, never told me, but I heard that he turned down the part because he had just finished in a flop with Donald Wolfit, and couldn't possibly be in two flops one after the other.

In a way Hubbard was the first part I had played since the war who had a definite vocation; being a detective is a vocation, and, since Dostoevsky, there is a place for detectives in the pantheon of fictional characters. *Crime and Punishment* is a wonderful study in the by-roads of evil, that space which covers the detection of evil. To sit in your police station, having gauged the nature of the criminal, assured that his vanity will eventually bring him within the magnet of your apparent disinterest, as the moth fatally comes once too near the candle, or to weevil through a patchwork of clues, adding up the sums to which the criminal alone fits; the linear and the mosaic commanding the tone of your style. There were many actors who possessed such a style – Harry Baur, Jouvet, Sidney Greenstreet (reference should always be upward) – that was at once commanding, threatening and still. Stillness was the clue; I played Hubbard with an intent irreverence. No fuss with sums.

The production was going to be inexpensive. I provided my own suit, and the set cost £500. I went into the stalls to see it being set up, as Hubbard's approaches and retreats from the flat door were important in the play.

I was watching it being set up with Jimmy Sherwood and Thane Parker in the stalls. They came to the door. Jimmy exploded. 'Look at

25

that door', he said, 'What does the carpenter think he's doing?' The door didn't fit. By at least, half an inch; you could see a streak of light at the foot of the door. Thane Parker was very bright. 'Wait a minute!' he said, 'Leave it like that. Then you'll be able to see the people come and go.' There was a silence.

So perhaps the most vivid physical aspect of the set was discovered, and duly exploited. I took a perverse delight in playing the part with my feet which must be unique in the history of the theatre. Approaching the door with a feigned heaviness, pausing for a moment, then ponderously turning round and walking slowly away, conscious that those inside who had not answered the doorbell would not only hear my footsteps as I walked away but see the shadow of my feet under the door. As the audience did too, holding their breath.

The play was a great success, and lasted a year. After the first night, Kenneth Tynan, the critic, pushed my dressing-room door open, and stammered 'Congratulations! Jolly good' his face nodding approval, though his head didn't seem to move. Later in the run, Vivien Leigh phoned Curigwen late one night to say that she and Larry had just seen the play and liked it enormously.

For the first time in my life, the line and mosaic of my being, if there was such an absurd thing, were being caught up in confusion. Success in the theatre generates an artificial activity which can easily smother the personal exploration. Indeed, among the gifts of an actor which are not generally recognized is that the immediacy of his performance, a very special achievement, is considered by the public as trivial and slight. This view is abetted by the actor, who does not wish his insights exposed and diminished; he would much prefer to be thought a fool. 'Marie, I loved the way you said . . .' 'Stop' said Dame Marie Tempest, 'I don't want to know.'

So might the dramatist feel about the admirers who like his 'conversation'. Being in a success, however, does give time for other things. Reading, for instance. I was getting absurdly caught up with Kierkegaard, feeling in an instinctive way that he held at least one key to the mass of doors that Hiroshima had opened. There was so much science to read. My professional life must revolve in some way round Shakespeare and Ibsen. I did not wish to do any more Shakespeare, but with Ibsen it was different. Ibsen is not a young man's playwright though more a young woman's; he is mainly a dramatist for the middle-aged and the old; his prose plays are a sort of biography.

Then there was the family. Curigwen and I are Christians, but we would not force our beliefs on the children, leaving it to them to choose. Indeed, one of the difficulties of the actor is that he cannot truly share his innermost thoughts with his wife. At least, I felt that in the great plays of Shakespeare and Ibsen, all I had to say was in the performance, but on the way to the performance I had my own testing to do, and to talk about it was a release to another person of a kind of energy I could not afford. If I was an artist, then the problems I had to solve were my own because I had recognized them as problems in the first place.

So I found in reading the Bible, which I was increasingly doing, caught up in the postwar impetus of biblical criticism. But I read Paul's letters and the rest of the New Testament not as a theologian but as an actor. When I read an Ibsen play I'm aware that it is the text I have to play. That text contains all the facts and words on which I have to build a character. It was not so when reading Paul's letters. Essential facts of the Gospels were left out of his consideration, which led me to wonder whether he had left them out deliberately, or even if he knew them. For instance he never mentions the virgin birth; that may not have been interesting in Paul's day, but it was going to become enormously important in the attempts to systematize Christianity. Again, a more significant omission to me, he disregards entirely the last words from the Cross, which is singular for one whose attachment to Christ was based partly on the fact that Christ was 'the cursed one'.

What was very clear to me was that all the discordance, and diversity of the first half of the twentieth century was concentrated into the Second World War, reaching a climax in the explosion at Hiroshima which not only pulped our cherished received beliefs into little bits, but violently scattered them over the uncertain surface of a world that was never at rest.

The play ran for a year. Then, as was the custom in those days, the West End cast was supposed to tour the dozen or so leading provincial theatres. This duly took place, after the cast had had a holiday. By this time Uncle Ivor, as we all called him, Curigwen's brother, had joined the RTZ company in Spain; he always chose his appointments with an eye on our family holidays. So in due course we all flew down to Madrid, then on to Seville, thence to Huelva and Punta Umbria, where the company had their summer chalets, one of which we occupied with, very importantly, domestic help for Curigwen – the girls were now ten and eight, Johnny six.

Punta, facing the Atlantic, is built on sand, the sea continually breaking into huge waves that provided a bubbling contrast to the unwavering warmth that boiled down from the sun; occasionally the heat flickered into a haze to show it was there.

In 1935, I had spent a holiday in Italy on the coast just south of Genoa, beneath the Carrara mountains, at a spot called Poveromo,

27

two miles from Forte dei Marmi. On the Sunday, when the inhabitants were at church, and I was alone on the beach, I thought I'd walk to Forte dei Marmi; it seemed quite safe, I was in my swimming shorts, bare feet, and a straw hat; there were clouds over the sun.

I had gone about half a mile when the clouds over the sun dissipated and for the next hour I endured its full heat on my back until I reached Forte dei Marmi.

The next three days I spent in the dark, blinds-drawn, tiled-floor bedroom of my modest pensione, smothered in olive oil, with that unique painful itch that is sunburn and with much Chianti.

Our daughters are very fair, and as I watched Curigwen cosset them from the great rollers they were delighting in, I knew they would not repeat my experience at Poveromo. They would respect the sun.

5 Restoring a Wholeness

When I'm away from home, touring with a play, or making a film, at least some of the books I take with me will reflect a concern about a problem that I might solve. The play was touring in the autumn so that I could guarantee plenty of opportunity for this study. It had to do with Kierkegaard, of course. Indirectly, Hiroshima, whose lesson I was trying to woo from the confusion of facts, evidence, and emotions surrounding the events.

Like Mary Stuart, Kierkegaard could have claimed 'in my end is my beginning'. In 1855, after thirteen years of the most intense self-analysis in European literature, Kierkegaard died, having just completed his last and most approachable work the *Attack on Christendom*, subtitled *The Instant*, a conclusion to his attack on the lack of spirit in his age, containing a blistering criticism of the bureaucracy of the Danish Church. Danish is a minor language, but Kierkegaards's skill in his use of it as a sceptical weapon ensured his fame outside his native country whose boundaries he crossed only four times, to visit Berlin.

The first to translate and publish the *Attack* were some publishers in Hamburg in 1862. Indeed, Germany was to be the channel for his thought to reach Europe. In his native land, the noted dramatic critic Georg Brandes displayed great enthusiasm for the work while his lectures on it revealed a very limited understanding (he never touches the *Fragments* or the *Postscript*) yet enough to pester his friend Ibsen to say how much he owed to Kierkegaard. The dramatist responded stiffly, 'I have read little of Kierkegaard, and understood less'.

Ibsen's response is revealing. Kierkegaard's polemic against society was easy to understand. The main body of his work because of its passionate novelty, more recalcitrant. Yet when recognition comes in the first decades of this century, it is experienced over a wide area of theology, philosophy and science, from Barth and Bultmann to Heidegger, Jean-Paul Sartre and the Danish physicist Niels Bohr and especially in the two most advanced capitals in Europe, Vienna and Paris. In Vienna, Karl Kraus seized on the polemic and repeated it in his own newspaper, *Die Fackel*, while Ludwig Wittgenstein thought Kierkegaard the most important thinker of the nineteenth century.

Yet I am not certain that any of those who were affected by Kierkegaard really understood him, as we, living under the shadow of Hiroshima, are compelled to understand him. As I sat in my digs in Akers Road, Manchester, over my supper after an evening performance at the Opera House, I asked myself why on earth I should think that I might understand him any better.

There were some reasons. Coming from under the cold, oyster skies of Aberdeenshire, there was a certain coldness in my heart and intellect, bred on the pain and poverty of my very young days, that engendered a subjective scepticism about the nature of truth; the 'truth' of the crowd, the screaming 'truth' of newspapers. I could see such gifts as I was born with gradually expanding in a corrosive society, and my mind was far too active to be satisfied with mere repetition. It needed an intellectual corrective to grasp what was new and seek out the areas where expansion was possible. Beyond all others, the actor's life is grounded on the mind and the memory. Behind Kierkegaard I thought I detected a light to guide me in this field.

There was again the theatre from which Kierkegaard had drawn the concrete pillars for his spheres of existence. Paradoxically, he had also condemned actors, like parsons, to be buried in unhallowed ground. I did not mind the ground, but I was not certain about my neighbours.

It was while I was studying Kierkegaard's spheres of existence in Manchester that I realized with a deadly sickness how much his work had suffered from its appropriation by philosophers and theologians. But why should I feel in a privileged position to refocus the work? Simply that the whole of European philosophy and to a great extent its theology derives from a difference of opinion that arose between Plato and Socrates in fifth-century Athens about the nature of thinking. The contentious issue was the purpose of theatre. Was the theatre a place of profound insights and delight as Socrates thought, or as Plato thought a distraction from the main business of life?

By the time Aristotle came to write his *Poetics*, the glory of the Athenian theatre had departed with the victory of Sparta, the players clearly scattered, and the dramatists demoralized. I am convinced that

Aristotle was writing about something he never experienced at its height. His *Poetics* is his tribute to one of the great Greek discoveries, language.

Following his study of Socrates in *The Concept of Irony*, Kierkegaard seems to be aware that he must begin with the Greeks. Examining Plato's notion of forms, and Aristotle's scheme of organisms, I think he found both unsatisfactory to explore the human condition in terms of personal identity and authentic behaviour. From early on the Greek figure that is to dominate his work is Socrates, whom he thought the greatest man who had ever lived. With the eventual conquest of Rome, European philosophy and theology has followed Plato and Aristotle. Now, Socrates has been reinstated and Greek theatre recognized as one of the great fountains of knowledge.

But there evolved in Europe over the centuries a notion that reached its climax in Descartes's mind-body division, the basis of which is that knowledge derived from the senses is uncertain and untrustworthy when compared with the objective, measurable accuracy of the mind. It has plagued European thinkers and is the ground for the great distrust of artists in our society.

Kierkegaard's spheres of existence is his attempt to restore wholeness to the human experience, as men and women exist in the situations in which they find themselves. These usually require a decision in one of three spheres which involve personal identity, the demands of society, and a response to the demands of sensuality. He calls these spheres the religious, the ethical and the aesthetic. It would have been simple but uncharacteristic for Kierkegaard to have described these spheres in the style of academic thought. More pertinent was to see these spheres as manifested in life or the next best thing, Greek tragedy. Hence the models for his three spheres are Agamemnon, Antigone and Don Juan. Agamemnon responds to the goddess's demand to sacrifice his daughter, Iphigenia. Antigone refuses to marry Haemon because the openness of marriage would require her to reveal the secret of Oedipus, her father, which she alone knows. And Don Juan? The choice of Don Juan as the model for the aesthetic was the masterstroke. For the aesthetic covers not merely the ranging experiences of sensuality, but the great world of creation as revealed in life and art through the imagination. It is one of the dominant facts of the Don Juan myth that for all his great triumphs in sex with women, we never see him in the act. It is left to our imagination.

A corollary of Kierkegaard's three spheres was his insistence that subjectivity is reality, subjectivity is the truth. He was a thinker pledged to the indirect.

31

The tour of *Dial M for Murder* finished, I returned home just before Christmas 1953, in time to take the children down to Brighton to the Royal Crescent Hotel where they didn't mind them sliding about on the polished floor when they weren't reading the *New Yorker*'s first twenty-five years, which was becoming very stained from use.

It was a real exercise in indirect communication that was now being intuitively practised more and more. No oughts, no judgements. An ethical silence like that of Antigone.

We returned to London for the new school term. I found myself very busy with radio and TV. It is extraordinary how much of what I did was forgettable, but that was part of the world that we were moving into; the instant, the immediate, the moment. We were living with them, but forgetting their history. We were at their mercy. But we needn't be.

Rudolph Cartier of the BBC sent me a play he was going to do on television, *Sacrifice to the Wind* (*Une Fille pour du vent*) by André Obey, translated by John Whiting. Would I play Agamemnon? Chance and necessity. I had no choice. By chance I received this play, it was necessary that I should play Agamemnon.

Obey, Jacques Copeau, whose pupil and nephew Michel Saint-Denis directed the Compagnie des Quinze, the producer Gaston Baty, the actors Charles Dullin and Louis Jouvet were revolutionizing European theatre. I remembered very clearly the impact of the Compagnie at the Savoy Theatre in Obey's *Le Viol de Lucrèce*. Marie-Hélène Dasté, sitting still on her Roman couch, Pierre Fresnay entering right, a dark creeping, snake-like figure, slowly moving towards Lucrèce – then the Narrator, A. Boverio, with hand upraised in warning, crying 'Tarquin! Tarquin!'

We forget how much the French theatre derives from the Greek, and transforms it. Oedipus and Agamemnon, the families that cling to the acropolis of Thebes and Mycenae provide through their dense family relationships the stories that some would dismiss as myths, on which generations of French dramatists have projected their dream of theatre. And yet, outside this doomed pair, another Greek Goddess intervenes, this time in Athens.

Phèdre is to the French what *Hamlet* is to the British, the difference in sex pointing to the stress of interest in the two races. Of the four main French actresses of my day, Marie Bell, Edwige Feuillère, Maria Casarès, and Madeleine Renaud, I have seen only the first two in Racine's play. Yet their difference was clear. Their playing of Phèdre's famous couplet was revealing:

32

Ce n'est plus une ardeur dans mes veines cachée;
C'est Vénus toute entière à sa proie attachée.
It is no longer a passion hidden in my veins;
It is the goddess Venus herself fastened on her prey.

Marie Bell played the lines expansively, as though the passion of the universe concentrated into Venus had absorbed her. Feuillère played them intensely, peering, as it were, at her entrails to seek out the goddess. It was a concrete example of one of the basic antinomies round which acting evolves, caught up beautifully in Kierkegaard's comment on style in diction. 'The objective accent falls on "what" is said, the subjective accent on "how" it is said.'

I did not think it possible to play Shakespeare so. Shakespeare is so caught up in the total objectivity of the world he is describing that to introduce an excessively individual tone would flaw the pattern of the tapestry. It was a matter of time. The beat, pulse and measure of a Shakespeare play demanded in its size a pressure in the playing if it was to be grasped whole; Racine's play was concentrated into few characters, leaving the dramatist room for his exquisite language. Indeed, given the nature of Madame de Maintenon, it was only the beauty of Racine's language that allowed him to approach such a subject that would otherwise have been censorable to the prurient French Court.

About this time I recorded Henri de Montherlant's play, *Port-Royal*, for radio. Again I was struck by the French capacity to combine intensity with a spacious elegance. Port-Royal was the Jansenist, Protestant enclave in French catholicism; it marked a dichotomy which is continually present in Christianity, whether Christ can be directly appropriated by the individual, or only through the mediation of the Church. The English solution is disappointingly undramatic; Anglicanism and Methodism, for all their beauty and enthusiasm, lack the tension of the theatre.

It was this division which fascinated the scientist/theologian Blaise Pascal when his sister, Jacqueline, joined the Jansenists. It was also the driving force that sustained St Augustine and Kierkegaard. For this reason Augustine's *Confessions*, Pascal's *Pensées* and Kierkegaard's *Journals* are the supreme day-books of Christianity.

Kierkegaard died in 1855. I had been doing a great deal of work on the BBC radio Third Programme (R3). I told them I had written to Walter Lowrie at Princeton University, inviting him to England to talk about his translations of the Danish thinker. He said he would be delighted to come; England was one of the few countries that had not taken to Kierkegaard; and the Third Programme agreed. It was disappointing when Bishop Johnston of the Cathedral of St John the Divine in New York wrote, asking if I knew what I was doing. Lowrie was a powerful man of 87. While his enthusiasm could not be doubted, his age must make me anxious. It was tragic when a little later I heard from Lowrie himself – his letter written in a spindly hand – that he'd had a stroke, compelling him to put off his visit to Europe. The conversion of England would have to wait.

It was in 1921, when I was thirteen, that I had my first experience of Greek drama. I was standing outside the classics room in the Aberdeen Grammar School, waiting for our teacher, imaginatively called Caesar, to turn up. Charlie Walker came up to me. He said he'd heard I was interested in acting. I was. Well, would I help the university in their production of *Oedipus Tyrannos* by Sophocles. It had been translated by the Greek professor, John Harrower, and was to be given in the Music Hall, Aberdeen. Would I be the Greek shepherd boy that leads on Tiresias, the blind seer? I said I would.

Some weeks later, in November, I found myself in an anteroom in the Music Hall before a blazing fire, applying bowl to my meagre body in the slender hope of persuading the audience that I was a Greek youth of the Mediterranean, and not Andy Cruickshank, him that's aye singing at Café-Chantants in a kilt, and in *The Dream of Gerontius*, or at His Majesty's Theatre in the company of the BNOC hearing his first *Meistersinger*, or watching Fred Terry and Matheson Lang and Sir Frank Benson and Martin Harvey.

Playing Creon was Eric Linklater, very swashbuckling, now like a painting himself, one of the first of the postwar generation at the university. He had wanted to be a doctor but had to settle for literature. He appeared very large and full of the authority of having seen great things. He had not yet written *Poet's Pub*. Meeting him later, he was really quite slight; my perspective had changed.

The new note that Obey's *Sacrifice to the Wind* introduced in the Iphigenia story was a young soldier for her; this was the background against which the great generals of the Greeks thrashed out their arguments with Calchas, the High Priest, on how to attract the wind to carry them to Troy. It was a very good play and translation, which Peter Hall noticed. He had just taken over the Arts Theatre for the 1955–56 season and would transfer *Sacrifice to the Wind* there in a double bill. The other play was *The Lesson*, the first Eugène Ionesco play to be presented in England. As is normal with our critics their attention was for the new; they write well with little penetration. Ionesco has faded, the Greeks are still with us.

Ever since my first glimpse of the Acropolis with the surprisingly off-centre Parthenon, the puzzle of the Greeks had occupied a layer of my sensibility. How to account for their enormous genius? Playing Agamemnon focused my mind on the nature of evolution in the theatre. In the *Oresteia* of Aeschylus, the murders of Agamemnon and Cassandra are the revenge which Clytemnestra takes for the sacrifice of her daughter, Iphigenia.

It was not Aeschylus's first play. The discoverer of tragedy demonstrated in his life how great dramatists work. First, the inheritance from the past; then as experience is gained in the medium, and expertness increases in the interpenetration of action and language, a stage is reached when technique matches original insight. So it is with Shakespeare, so with Ibsen, so it first was with Aeschylus. Aeschylus's genius was to marry the past, history as seen through the Homeric classics, the *Iliad* and the *Odyssey*, with the increasing social awareness of fifth-century Athens, particularly in the *Oresteia* which follows the guilt of Clytemnestra from the *Agamemnon* into the *Libation Bearers* and the *Eumenides*. History showed immaculate taste in preserving the *Oresteia*, the only trilogy from the first great period of civilization.

To anyone with a gift for the theatre, like Sophocles and Euripides, the new insights were enormously fruitful, especially at a time when Mycenae and Thebes were siding with Sparta against Athens. Yet such was the ambiguity of the historical sources that the dramatists had enormous freedom to improvise. Thus Euripides could begin with the Agamemnon story at the port of Aulis, and carry it on after the Aeschylus play to Tauris where Iphigenia, like Isaac from the hands of Abraham, is transported; swearing vengeance on the first Greek to visit the Crimea, who is, with proper Greek irony, her brother, Orestes.

It seemed that the great field of Greek myth, the result of the Greek inquiry into the nature of identity, was spread out before the dramatist for his selection, ranging from Troy to Athens, embracing such conflicting characters as Antigone and Philoctetes.

The event which spurred this renewed estimation of the Greek achievement was the publication of John Chadwick and Michael Ventris's *Documents in Mycenean Greek* (1956). Darwin's *The Origin of Species* of 1859 had released a great leap forward in the sciences, not least in archaeology and anthropology. In the 1870s Heinrich Schliemann had uncovered Troy and Mycenae; at the turn of this century Sir Arthur Evans revealed the glory of Knossos with the abundant clay tablets that had been baked in the volcanic eruption that destroyed the palace; tablets with their signs, an inventory of the goods and chattels of the palace. Resistant to Evans, the tablets were deciphered by an Anglo-

Greek architect, Ventris, while John Chadwick linked the discovery with the earliest Greek language in *The Decipherment of Linear B* (1958).

To an actor the discovery was mind-boggling. Centuries before any other race, the Greeks were speaking a language they could only write down in signs. When deciphered, the language was composed of syllables, that is vowels and consonants, the ground of all spoken language. And the language was a description of things, not feelings. They were to come later. Language was discovered to describe a tripod, the number of bulls, the flagons of wine, the contents of the larder, the articles of worship but not the worship itself.

And it was in verse. When Ventris told the Classical Association in Copenhagen of his discoveries, he opened the meeting with a slide showing on the left the sign of a tripod, on the right the word t-i-r-i-p-o-d-e. The meeting burst into applause. They were applauding the discovery; the actor would have gone further and recognized two iambic feet.

It was foolish not to have thought of it before. Verse had to precede prose because it conformed more easily to the pulse of the voice, and the sounds that through the pulse could be communicated more fluently to someone else who had a voice, and so the first actors came into being. Those people who had voices and memory to remember the sounds. The discovery would have seemed absurd – just a few actors who could speak? Was there previously a great silence? No, it wasn't like that. It is a characteristic of evolution that initial discoveries are simple with an enormous capacity to proliferate swiftly. Once the sounds were discovered, they were available to everyone. That some were better than others is proved by the origin of narrative, and the need for actors with unusual gifts, with a voice that matched their memory, to entertain and move with stories that we now regard as myths but when casually invented and delivered gave coherence to the first wayward pangs among individuals seeking identity and a warmth in an emerging group awareness.

Like Ibsen, Greek tragedy is not a prime necessity for English audiences, so I was soon available to return to the Westminster Theatre for another thriller, *Dead on Nine*. This was to carry me through the rest of 1955 and into 1956.

I was beginning to be haunted by the spectre of the actor, with his unique mind and memory, being able to inhabit different people in places as separate as Athens, Copenhagen and London. With the modern resources of radio, television and film he could do it in a weekend.

36

6 Peter Daubeny

The next year was to be occupied one way or another with the activities of the impresario Peter Daubeny. An Adonis of a creature, it might have been Rupert Brooke straying into a different war in which Daubeny had lost an arm. He had a passion that he was unable to bridle for all movement that led to the theatre. If he ever did, I never saw him act; but I can't believe he did, he didn't have the actor's uncertainty. His mind, at this time in the fifties, was totally preoccupied with his great project, the World Theatre seasons. However, in the intervals between exploring the lower Himalayas and like places for new theatre to squeeze into his programme, he contrived to mount a play by Hugh Mills, *The House by the Lake*, at the Duke of York's Theatre, in which I was asked to play with Flora Robson.

The play was produced in May 1956 and settled in for a longish run. There was time to absorb Peter's other activities. I don't think he was inspired by any particular ideology. His passion for the theatre was for its diversity, not the nature of its roots. Yet his choice of companies for the World Theatre season at the Palace Theatre revealed, if it was deliberate, a profound understanding of the main trends in European theatre; and this at a time when the native theatre was in the doldrums.

The centre of the season was held by two great European companies of the time, the Berliner Ensemble and the Renaud-Barrault company. The main productions of the companies were *Mother Courage* by Bertolt Brecht, and *Christophe Colombe* by Paul Claudel.

For centuries the spectre of Shakespeare had loomed behind English dramatists as an inspiration or a prohibition, inspiring an example which was never realized, or by its sheer size inhibiting any succession.

37

The verse plays that Irving had commissioned for the Lyceum were woeful; and such poets as had written plays, like Dr Johnson, Shelley and Browning, were completely barren of theatre awareness. None of them realized what the theatre was for. Faced with the question, the prompt answer was always – to entertain. The retreat saved any further investigation; even the notion of delight was excluded.

My familiarity with Ventris deepened my notions of the line and the mosaic engendered by *Hamlet* and *King Lear*. The wonder of the fifth-century Greek world overwhelmed me; particularly when I realized that it was grounded in language in the theatre; there was scarcely an island in the Aegean that had not produced its genius, like Democritus and Hippocrates, to peer with fresh eyes at some aspect of life, to map the ground on which we still base our lives.

The building matter of life is the molecule; it provides the structure for growth. My first molecule was derived from fifth-century Athens; there men assembled and were seized by an insight, a technique, an energy (my molecule!). As I saw it, Aeschylus is the father of tragedy, not merely because he is the first to use language dramatically, but on account of his perception that the situation at Mycenae between Agamemnon and Clytemnestra (which does not appear in Homer's *Iliad*), contained the elements that fired his imagination to a new kind of song, like a goat song intruding irrationally among the other domestic sounds that were familiar and acceptable. For tragedy is not acceptable. In Homer's epics, the stories are about what x did to y. Greek tragedy seizes imperishably on the consequences that lead to the one great inevitability, death. In so doing it provided a limit to what was possible in the human condition, and a source for the Greek saying, 'Nothing too much!'

Fifth-century Athens was adept at evolving the institutions required for a city-state. Thus the areopagus (law court), the agora (meeting place), but most importantly the Parthenon (temple of Athena), and the Theatre of Dionysus. Between them they provide the first model for social organization, the technique of blending diversity into a unity. Given the speed with which they replaced the statuary of the Acropolis that had been destroyed by the Persians, the energy generated by the first great period of civilization was apparent.

I had experienced before the problem presented to English dramatists by Brecht and Claudel. English life is bounded by politics and finance. The politics is pragmatic, lacking an ideology. Since Adam Smith, the husbandry of the country was everyone's concern. Thus, in a climate where everything like the Empire was disintegrating, the only institution that unsurprisingly showed growth was the Stock Exchange.

38

In the first decades of the century, when a choice between Ibsen and Chekhov was first presented to English playwrights, the extremities of Marxism and Catholicism were still muted in ignorance. Between the wars, the plight of Chekhov's characters were too close to the English experience to be avoided. Ibsen was boring even when understood. Thus British playwrights like Ronald Mackenzie and Rodney Ackland were hailed as of the school of Chekhovian naturalism. There was an invitation in Chekhov to self-indulgence and self-pity which was not always avoided. The excuse for it, it was so beautiful. The dominant tone in the work of English (and Scottish playwrights like James Bridie) was naturalism. How did it differ from a realist tone? What was realism in the theatre?

Daubeny was providing a choice between two kinds of European realism, between Christianity and Marxism. Both claimed to be the reflection of a final truth, once revealed. Art is the solution to problems that cannot be solved in any other way. Zhdanov's prescription to the 1934 Writers' Congress in Russia of Socialist Realism as the solution for the problem of the Communist artist was debilitating except for lively minds like Brecht's. Epic theatre was acceptable. Homer was one of Marx's favourite authors, Berlin was a long distance from Moscow, and the word 'epic' contained great possibilities.

Brecht exploited his location and intelligence to great advantage. He was too remote from immediate Moscow surveillance, and the Leninist element in Communism was diluted by his experiences with the Frankfurt school of Marxist philosophers, notably Theodor Adorno, and in America. He had a great admiration for the teamwork of English actors. His notion of alienation was through paradox to heighten those strains he wished the audience to absorb.

I took Flora Robson to see *Mother Courage* one matinée. At the famous moment in the play when Courage (Helene Weigel) is bending over her dead son and tossing her head back, but not wishing to reveal her relationship, opens her mouth to emit no sound, Flora hissed in my ear, 'I refuse to do the actress's work for her!'

In harmony with the Christian claim of universality, Claudel was committed to total theatre, a view which suited Barrault's great gifts. The play opened with a short film clip showing a globe and two great hands moulding the universe. In portraying Christophe Colombe's tortuous voyage over the Atlantic, all the arts of theatre, design, music, mime, sound and sight were ravished as eventually, through the storms of the sea, the cry went up from the watch, 'Terre! Terre!' The language was verse.

English dramatists had little difficulty in showing which dramatist they preferred. Apart from T. S. Eliot and Christopher Fry, who were already committed to verse in the theatre, the new fashion was socialist realism but of a kind not to be confused with the romantic glow in which Russian writers were adjured to see the state. The main practice of the new realism was to be found at the Royal Court Theatre where George Devine was struggling to re-establish something of the excitement that Shaw had seen in Barker's theatre at the beginning of the century.

I had been directed by George Devine at the Old Vic, where he shared the production of *The Tempest* with Marius Goring. He was one of those academics that were to flow like lava from Cambridge and overwhelm the theatre. The source was suspect – Shakespeare was not a University wit. Devine slavishly followed Michel Saint-Denis, whose talent had not greatly inspired me, even to the extent of smoking a similar pipe, and carrying about with him a similar exercise book with his notes for the production. Both had similar difficulties in deciphering their notes.

But he was a magnet of a sort. He attracted new playwrights who unfortunately were soon exhausted and did not provide that continuous vision which sustains the theatre. The theatre is not like painting and music. Renaissance painters seem to sprout everywhere in Italy with an equal brilliance. In the nineteenth century music laps over the frontiers of Europe, conjoined in the romantic glow of their differing colours. But great theatre happens very infrequently because the great dramatist is unpredictable. Shakespeare, almost casually, provides the nucleus round which the Elizabethan and Jacobean theatre revolves. Paradoxically, Ibsen did not provide the centre for a great theatre, as Chekhov did for the producer Konstantin Stanislavsky at the Moscow Art Theatre.

The flaw in the Brecht and Claudel plays was that they were all about subjects drawn from the past. At least *Look Back In Anger* had a contemporary theme; and there was some vigour in John Osborne's writing, but it was generalized. The tone of resentment was never focused into a specific knot, unlike Ibsen who in his mature period always binds his plays to people with vocations in corrupt society. Since corruption is continually present, so are those who, wittingly or unwittingly, practise it, the professionals, those with vocations.

However, what gave particular point to the Osborne play with its implied comment on English decline was the outbreak in October 1956 of the Anglo-French escapade in the eastern Mediterranean after Egypt had seized the Suez canal.

It is part of the existential armour that society is a whole like the tapestry of Bayeux or the Parthenon frieze, in which the actions of men interpenetrate the world of nature and society. Unfortunately, and this was one of the notes in the Osborne play, England was still a hierarchy, doomed to the maintenance of the status quo, committed to a specialization in politics, and perhaps more disastrous, in education, creating a society in which people were unable to synthesize.

The full impact of the Suez disaster was mitigated by the almost uncanny near-simultaneity of the Russian invasion of Hungary on some specious ideological ground. Both incursions were localized; the example of Hiroshima still sufficient to stimulate second thoughts.

Suez was left to the specialists, to the Prime Minister, Eden and his French counterpart, Guy Mollet. There is little point in arguing the rights and wrongs of the wretched affair, except to note that temporarily retired ex-President de Gaulle stayed well clear of it, and Eden had stomach pains which caused his early retirement, and, as is customary in England when solving problems of failure, his elevation to the House of Lords.

The *House by the Lake* ran well over a year, and after the usual tour of the provinces I returned to London and a period of fascinating work. It was a period when West End successes were transferred rapidly to television, and after I'd done Barrett, the father, in *The Barretts of Wimpole Street*, I played the dentist in Graham Greene's *The Complaisant Lover* (1957), and the sculptor in Robert Bolt's *The Tiger and the Horse* (1960). The point about these plays was that, while they were all sensitively written, they fell into the category of naturalism. While contemporary, they yet lacked the profundity of groping round the roots of society.

I was beginning to feel the lack in London of centres of interest, though Olivier and Gielgud were obviously fulfilled at the Royal Court. Of the new playwrights only Samuel Beckett and Harold Pinter were interesting for a specific reason. For the first time in the modern British theatre, language was being used as though it had a vitality of its own and did not need the support of characters with vocations in everyday jobs. It was as though Beckett and Pinter sitting down before an empty sheet of paper, could write a sentence that could generate a life of its own for the dramatist to weave into a play.

I could understand Beckett's position. He had worked with Joyce in France. Once Joyce had completed *Dubliners* and *Portrait of the Artist as a Young Man*, he had as it were fixed his position in the world of objects, and was ready to contemplate the inward journey of *Ulysses*. The *Iliad* would not do as a model; the *Odyssey* provided the pattern for his day's journey through Dublin. It was for this inwardness that he had hailed

41

Ibsen, and it was the tone of the novel in France first sensed by Stendhal in the 1830s, then nourished by Gustave Flaubert, to emerge fully in every sense in Marcel Proust.

This inwardness was to become the dominating apprehension as the world of objects lost its certainty. In this cloud of unknowing that was the individual imagination, words were the only succour Beckett did not need to explain his plays; they were of the moment. But that moment of time was the only space in which they could live, the only space and time in which the audience could receive them. It was inevitable that he would eventually write a play enacted only by a mouth, *Not I*. I do not think Beckett realized that he was the first writer in a world created by science. It was a pity that the Irish had appropriated Beckett, but it was a relief that he also wrote in French.

What I found in Beckett that was lacking in the successful plays I was appearing in was a reaching out towards a new kind of reality that had not yet formed. Though we had been given the components, we had not yet resolved a synthesis. Indeed, I doubted if a synthesis could ever be formed except on a temporary basis, for the fundamental fact that permeated all life and art was that everything moves, the universe is never at rest.

Of more immediate concern in this maelstrom was the division that was reappearing between England and the Continent which the failure of Suez had sharpened. De Gaulle was with typical realism fashioning a concord with Germany and Italy. The Marshall Plan was proving enormously successful – which was scarcely surprising, given the nature of the Germans. France above all was striding towards a new identity. It was as though the main countries of Europe tempered by failure, had been offered a lifeline towards forging a new identity, relieved of a hierarchy that was shackling movement in England.

Repetition was the interest of English hierarchy, and it was the interest on which the hierarchy was to founder. The continent was proving that the rejection of hierarchy did not mean an uncritical acceptance of the new. Time was becoming increasingly important as it was in physics. The instant, the now, had a history; the task was to recognize what kind of history.

In 1919, when he had split the nitrogen atom at the Cavendish laboratory in Cambridge, Ernest Rutherford thought there was no future in it; Arthur Eddington, on the other hand, thought it would be either the salvation or destruction of mankind.

There was, of course, a history to the splitting of the atom, dating back to James Clerk Maxwell's equations of 1864–73 defining a new reality, the field, the electromagnetic field that Michael Faraday had with wonderful intuition divined from his observation of the behaviour of magnets, filings and electric batteries. The most powerful force in the universe, greater than gravity, that Einstein had caught in his Special Theory of Relativity. Science had its layers of revelation, just like human beings.

Suddenly, one weekend I was phoned up to say that a new kind of theatre was opening in Croydon, what they called a theatre-in-the-round, the Pembroke, and they wished me to play in the opening play. Would I read it? I said yes. The play was *Inherit the Wind*.

My life as an actor, now that the family was established, was being experienced on two levels. Hubbard, the detective in *Dial M for Murder*, was characteristic of the surface level; the deeper level had been established first in Shakespeare in *Hamlet* and *King Lear*, touched on in New York in *Hedda Gabler*, and now was about to resume.

Although the play (by Jerome Lawrence and Robert E. Lee) was good enough, it was elevated beyond its level by the nature of the subject, the conflict between the biblical explanation of life and Darwin's *The Origin of Species*. The occasion was the teaching in 1925 at a school in Tennessee of Darwin's theory in an area of America that was fundamentalist Christian. The arguments hovered round, and still exist, on the literalness of the Bible texts.

It is an aspect of the religious imagination that holy texts, including miracles that lie outside the laws of nature, have a validity that preserves them from ordinary scrutiny. This is part of the generalisation known as faith. It occurs also in Communism where, following Marx, the ground of hope is that the state will wither away sometime in the future into a harmony where the individual will enjoy the freedom to create his vision of beauty. It is called by some uncharitable critics Utopia. And in order that the vision may not be tarnished, it justifies any cruelty, any persecution, any darkness at noon, on those who might be deemed to threaten the vision now.

I found more and more, as the concepts about the theatre and life were flooding in on me, my mind was not only registering my experience in layers as it were a library with its shelves, or a gallery with its pictures, but also at the same time acting as a sieve allowing into my consciousness only those pictures that coincided with my external experience. This movement in my mind was given solid ground in *Inherit the Wind* in that behind the characters of fiction were not only real people, but people of some substance. Thus the three main characters were, in life, Clarence Darrow, the great Chicago lawyer of apparently lost causes, William Jennings Bryan, the fundamentalist who had unsuccessfully stood three times for the presidency of the United States, and H. L. Menken from Baltimore, arguably the most radical journalist of his day. The argument that had engaged such participants was ultimately about the nature of life and experience, about the nature of knowledge. Did life change with knowledge, or was it an endless repetition of a fixed, received knowledge of the past?

When Darrow, with an immediate daring, put Bryan into the witness stand, his intention was clearly to question him about this literalness; which was surfacing again at this moment in theological circles in England when the play was being performed.

In England, the question, the myth of God incarnate, was dividing the ecclesiastical establishment, raising tempers to a level that had hardly been experienced since the Reformation. The tempers in Tennessee were all on one side, prompted by the fear that their God was being hijacked away from them. Few sympathized with Darwin and his immediate exponents, John T. Scopes, the teacher, and Darrow, the advocate.

Two forms of revelation, secular (Darwin) and divine (the Bible), were being examined together for the first time in a law court! *Inherit the Wind* was not a great play, but this contingent aspect of the entertainment was entirely disregarded, even among critics – who, like Harold Hobson, a Christian Scientist, and of all people, T. C. Worsley, were insufferably patronizing.

For the first time in the theatre, I felt in touch with two of the most fundamental problems of the day; in a modest way, art was solving problems that could not be solved in any other way. As to our critics, I could only conclude that their uncertainty arose from the fact that while half of them may have known about God, the other half tended towards evolution.

I decided that I should not fall between two stools; I would feed on both. I was encouraged along this path because, while playing in the round, before a performance, I became acutely aware of a Euclidean dimension in my mind that had not revealed itself so openly when I was playing in a proscenium-arch theatre.

Actors never talk about the discipline they use before a performance to tune themselves for their appearance. We are creatures of instinct and many, no doubt, feel no need for such preparation. Others may have contrived their own private systems.

Unless you are playing at one of our national theatres, there is never really enough rehearsal for the actor to absorb entirely the part, the other person, that he is playing. I mean that total absorption of the other person down to the nervous system that provides the impulse for action. I was coming to the conclusion that it is only really great plays that provide a partial shadow from which the actor can evolve a whole substance; Ibsen never tells us of Hedda Gabler's eating habits or Judge Brack's taste in music. Though if he did, we might well say, 'That's exactly what I expected!'

Before the performance at Croydon every night, I would sit down quietly some ten minutes before the play started, close my eyes, then draw a geometric figure in my mind of my moves in the play. I had such control over this reflection that I could accelerate it, or slow it down, according to feeling. The origin of theatre in the round is the Greek orchestra, the megaron (hall) of the kings of Mycenae that the Greek dramatists adapted and transformed. And so, sitting in London, I would surround my mind sometimes with the spectators at a performance in the theatre of Dionysus in Athens. It worked just as well. I still use this discipline in a proscenium-arch theatre, but somehow it is shackled. The Greek orchestra had wonderful reverberations; this little O, the world, the mind.

The play was successful enough to encourage George Fearon, our publicity man, to persuade two young men, Peter Bridge and John Gale, to dive into management. We had a modest run at the St Martin's Theatre.

One of the reverberations of the play, as we were moving into a permissive society, was the discreet sensuality that pervaded it. Questions about the nature of sex and its practice never arose, though it was the origin of much of the passionate protest in the play, in which an explosion was prevented by the legal procedure.

In the plays between *The House by the Lake* and *Inherit the Wind*, only two prompted some sharp thought on sex in the theatre, and out of it: Shaw's *Candida* and Hugh Ross Williamson's *Queen Elizabeth*. Both were with Edith Evans, and were recordings for the BBC. In the first I played her husband, Morel; in the second her lover, Leicester.

From 1929 when I started as a professional actor, the condition sexually of the London theatre has been a hothouse of mixed and harmonious communions.

Between the wars, when uncertainty was beginning to be felt in every dimension of society, it was hardly unexpected that some chaos should occur in that art which dealt most intimately with human relations. That love that dared not speak its name, which had caused Oscar Wilde such pain, was appearing overtly in the theatre; I played Clark, the defending counsel in a play, *Oscar Wilde* by Leslie and Sewell Stokes, about the trial, produced in 1936 at the Gate Theatre – a private theatre.

At the same theatre, paradoxically, with Reginald Beckwith I adapted Aristophanes's *Lysistrata*, playing the Spartan herald in Scots. Both plays were banned at the time. Sex, whether practised promiscuously or denied, was reprehensible. Freud was spreading everywhere, even into the theatre. At the Old Vic during the rehearsals of *Othello*, after the epilepsy scene, Olivier once kissed Richardson – who was much discomfited and warned him not to do it again. During *Hamlet*, Guthrie had consulted Ernest Jones, Freud's biographer.

There was much misunderstanding about the nature of sex. We can be fairly sure that when neanderthal man began to explore his body he quickly recognized those parts of it which gave him most excitement. Sex was so easy and unaccountable, to say nothing about the devious way in which it could be practised. And, when successful, it gave much pleasure. Alas, that could not always be predicted. It is a great pity that when Freud was writing *The Interpretation of Dreams* (1900), Karl Kraus did not give him a copy of Kierkegaard's *The Concept of Dread*.

Homosexuals were spreading into the management of the English theatre with interesting consequences. That they were efficient there was no doubt, but there was more to the theatre than efficiency. The point was, had they the right kind of dread?

It was said by some, and I had no way to disprove it, that Flora Robson and Edith Evans had beautiful bodies. I had been husband to both of them – in plays. That people should have seen them thus was a legacy from the nineteenth century when sensuality was hidden in the imagination, along with such lumber as sex and the aesthetic; in that corner of the mind where, as Kierkegaard saw, was lodged 'the natural and sensual man's method of parrying the ethical claim'.

Anyway, Evans and Robson were big girls, Curigwen was slight. The big girls had no children, Curigwen had three (conceived at an age not quite as advanced as the biblical Abraham's Sarah, but old enough to plead relief from such traumas). Unlike the Father in the Strindberg play, I was certain they were mine. Resistance to the big girls was easy; my ethical relationship was secure.

Out of the blue I was asked to see Anthony Mann, an American film director. Rough spoken in contrast to his sensitivity as a film director, he talked about making a great Spanish epic – in Spain. I was really having the riches of two worlds, an intellectual involvement with how life began, and the prospect of another visit to Spain.

7 *The Lady from the Sea*

In our first visit to Spain we had just passed through Madrid on our way south, to Huelva, on the Atlantic coast, six years earlier. Now I'd be leaving the family again. The modern theatre is such a diverse spontaneous activity, unable to provide that constant ground on which families rely as a background for growth and extension. The children were now in their early teens, their education path settled. None of them showed any talent for music requiring a special care, but I found them enormously attractive. Curigwen was their immediate bridge into the family consciousness. I was a rather remote figure of fun in the background who could always be related to a New Yorker cartoon. They knew of my interests, but didn't applaud them. If we gave them an example they showed no haste to follow it. They were what all children should be, a corrective.

In short, in a world continually in flux my family provided a certainty, a nucleus round which I could revolve like an electron. Even to the extent of changing orbits as I was doing now. Why did the return to Spain raise in me such expectancy? It was not the interest of playing the father of one of the age's most glamorous actresses, Sophia Loren. History stepped in; the memory of Italian films immediately after the war, the new realism, Vittorio De Sica, Rossellini's *Open City*.

But my memory went further back to January 1939, the first night of the Old Vic tour of the Mediterranean, the tour that was to turn Europe's face away from the vulgarities of Hitler and Mussolini. Opening in Lisbon with Sheridan's *The Rivals*, I was playing O'Trigger; as I first entered in the second act, I was passing a breath of time on the portico of the National Theatre, overlooking the central square,

47

which was empty except for the flowersellers under their minute umbrel-la-shaped trees, their baskets of gardenias glistening white from the falling rain. Suddenly I heard a commotion coming from the river Tagus, and there burst into the square a rabble of young men, their shirts torn, their brown skins gleaming in the rain, straining forward like revolutionaries in a Géricault painting behind a red and gold banner, shouting 'Arriba España!' It was 26 January, the day that Barcelona fell, the day that marked the end of the Spanish Civil War.

There is about the English a continual tendency to hover towards the moderate. However extreme their passion, they find it difficult to sustain over a period. It was difficult for me to understand the emotions they so clearly felt for both sides in the Spanish Civil War. For if ever a war was fought from extreme positions, it was in Spain. The war marked, too, a resurgence of the Spanish saints; St John of the Cross and St Teresa of Avila. *The Dark Night of the Soul* was a book for the pocket like A. E. Housman's *A Shropshire Lad*, and the saint of Avila was a more wholesome mystic than her French namesake of Lisieux. I now left for Spain with some curiosity.

I shared a flat with Gary Raymond in the Torre de Madrid, a recently built high-rise block that everyone swore would soon collapse. Others had been known to. But it was high, and we had views over the Manzanares towards the Casa de Campo, landmarks of the Civil War. History embroiders places with wisps of memory that tear at the heart. I was often plagued with stillness in Madrid, especially as, in the square outside our flat, there was a fountain surrounding a bronze figure of Don Quixote.

The early days in Madrid were spent preparing me for battle. My hair was flecked with grey which now had to be erased. I grew a beard which also had to be turned to charcoal. Within a few years I'd experienced the wide spectrum of activity that science had opened up for the artist. Theatre, proscenium and open stage, electronic, radio and television, and now the large screen. I had played a crook, a dentist, a sculptor, a lawyer, a parson. I was a man of the professions.

And the film itself held an expanding fascination. Like *King Lear, El Cid* is about two families, with their appendages. There the similarity ends. For while *King Lear* anticipates the modern world – it was written the same year in which Bacon's *The Advancement of Learning* was published, 1605 – Corneille's *Le Cid*, one of several literary sources for the film, is the summit of the medieval practice of courtly love, focused into a situation of great dramatic intensity, the expulsion of the Moors from Spain. Where in *Lear* the action through suffering embraces all humanity and the scraping away of illusion to a naked identity, *El*

48

Cid is concerned with the embroideries and tricks of hierarchical power games surrounded by the glow of romantic love. It is the great paradox of romantic love as expressed in the medieval poetry of the troubadours and in the twelfth-century *Poema del Cid* to adorn verse with a measure and grace that is its own intellectual fulfilment. The notion that such an intense expression of love should ever be consummated in the flesh was repugnant to the poet. Troubadour verse is the first example in Europe of the painful appropriation of a truth without corroding it. St John of the Cross had been given some precepts.

I was the head of one family, Michael Hordern that of the other, Loren was my daughter, Charlton Heston (the Cid) his son. We were in conflict which would ultimately bring Heston and me to fight it out. The film was proceeding with grandeur and dash when we heard that Loren was to do another film so the schedule was altered in order that her work with us would be completed in time.

For almost a fortnight I was incarcerated in the Real Madrid Football Club gymnasium with an Italian fencer who never seemed to tire, getting accustomed to a broadsword and mapping out the routine of a fight to a death that was unpleasantly extended. Eventually, Heston and I were landed in a very large, pillared set with Anthony Mann, our Italian tutor – and Loren. For days, it seems, we rehearsed, fought, and filmed this duel until I was vanquished. It was an agonizing process. The odds were clearly against me, until I lay dying and Loren took me in her arms, when the clouds suddenly lifted. For two days I lay in her arms while the scene was filmed.

I had some years before played Brackenbury, the governor of the Tower of London, in Olivier's 1955 film of *Richard III*. The scene was with Gielgud playing Clarence in a nightmarish state before his murder. Olivier then had purred lovingly over the camera, coaxing it to give of its best for this great colleague of his, with whom he had once doubled the parts of Romeo and Mercutio.

Now that scene was to repeat itself, with different characters. Loren had some of the same facility as Flora Robson. I always felt with Flora that I had only to murmur the word 'Titanic' and her eyes would immediately fill with tears. So now it was with Loren and Anthony Mann. Crouched over the camera like Olivier, he would whisper, 'It's your father, Sophia. You're never going to see him again. Just think o'that. (pause) Got it?' As a slight noise echoed through the pillared hall, 'Jesus, what is this? Central Park Station? All right, settle down everywhere. Let's have it quiet.'

During the interruption I would open my eyes, and there were the tears, glistening on her cheek. Frequently, leading actresses have blemishes like bad breath or a skin complaint; it's a complementary part of their energy. But Loren had no blemishes except one. Her beauty was exhaustible. I had begun my reclining days feeling something like a French troubadour; after two days I finished like one, unconsummated and glad of it.

The film was notable for a new kind of financing with which I was unacquainted. Sometimes a rumour would filter through from the Spaniards. There were doubts about being paid. Then, in time, a grain ship from America would anchor in Barcelona, and there would be a sigh of relief. The producer Samuel Bronson apparently had done a deal with the American and Spanish governments by which the Americans would supply grain which the Spanish would pay for in facilities, while still retaining the distribution rights of the film.

It sounded eminently sensible, so long as the films were of *El Cid*'s calibre. It signalled a technical condition that was bound to increase as long as the lesson of Hiroshima was remembered and no war broke out. The days of a Cunard financing Sir Thomas Beecham, or a Barry Jackson or Miss Horniman singly financing a Birmingham Repertory Theatre or an Abbey Theatre in Dublin were over. Society was growing and increasing in diversity, creating problems in finance that were no longer soluble with crumbs from the rich man's table.

Expectations in every aspect of human existence were increasing, inviting a completely new mode of economic thought, and a deeper moral awareness in its practice. Europe was being challenged to rise to a new level of relationship, to divest itself of memory and see itself engaged in a new adventure. The theatre was there for all to see within its closed walls, walls that were not expandable.

I had two weeks in Madrid while Sophia was finishing off her work with the rest of the cast. During these two weeks I took the opportunity with other members of the cast, who like me were unneeded, to explore the towns round Madrid, provided they had cars. I did not drive at that time. There were four towns I wished to see, Toledo, Segovia, Avila and (furthest away) Salamanca, and two weeks to visit them. I had my reasons; El Greco at Toledo, the Roman aqueduct at Segovia, St John of the Cross and St Teresa at Avila, and at Salamanca the university where Miguel de Unamuno had once been rector at the outbreak of the Civil War. He had previously learned Danish and discovered Kierkegaard.

The visits were spread over two weeks. On the days between I would drift down to the Prado and stare for hours at the El Grecos, the Goyas and the Velázquezes. At the end of the two weeks, what did I feel about it? I was looking at a span of history that was uniquely Spanish, beginning with Rome and stretching through the dark ages to the medieval world and on to the day before yesterday. Had I been in France, Germany or indeed England, it would have been much the same. The same pattern was repeated in the nations of Europe, with their own national differences. A Rembrandt in one place, an El Greco in another. As a wartime staff officer I had had to begin an appreciation with the letters GLD, the general line of direction. All the arts – painting, sculpture, music, drama – were all represented in the courts of Europe in their various ways; sometimes some losing touch, while others steamed ahead, then a scurrying to catch up, and a leap ahead. Art was a constant reference in a continually changing world. Art itself changed, but very slowly.

I was poised in a most illuminating situation, comparing Shakespeare with Corneille. One of the many strains that go to make their plays was the example of the troubadour. Long before Byron and Scott in literature, and the great romantic composers from Beethoven to Strauss set their mark on the nineteenth century, the troubadours of France had defined the romantic in its purest sense. From this Shakespeare starts in *Love's Labour's Lost*, and proceeds to the great tragedies of *Hamlet* and *King Lear*, Corneille pauses with the poets of the Pléiade, with Ronsard and du Bellay. Shakespeare anticipates Newton, Racine is a contemporary of Descartes.

Comparing Spain and France at this moment was illuminating. Twenty-one years after the end of the Civil War, Spain was at peace, but uneasy. There was no governing idea holding the people together. The cruelties perpetrated during the Civil War, neighbour on neighbour, were too deep to be glossed over, particularly under a regime that projected no vision.

Five years after the failure of Suez, France, under President de Gaulle, had been presented with a programme that every Frenchman could subscribe to. Nothing less than the nation itself, France. France must be seen as independent and secure. During the dark years of the Occupation, France's leading philosopher, Jean-Paul Sartre, had composed his major work, *L'Être et le néant* (*Being and Nothingness*). There is much to disagree with in Sartre's work; but in one respect his message was clear to those intellectuals like André Malraux and Raymond Aron who surrounded de Gaulle. He seemed to be saying that out of nothingness we create our identity and discover our authentic selves.

The means were at hand, nuclear fission. France must have its own defence force, and control the power for its industries. The *Force de frappe* provided the cover, and the nuclear power stations eighty per cent of the energy that French industry required. I do not know any French politician who would now abandon these projects. Unlike England, where a failure in conceptual thinking had created a favourable climate for generalized abstractions that mollified any uneasy feelings that we might have lost touch with reality.

I felt now that the extremity I had experienced in Spanish art, and that was reproduced in the temper of the people, had taken its place in my European pantheon. Exhausted by the acquisition, I was tired and longed for home and the ease of familiar faces.

Fortunately, when Sophia left, Tony Mann ploughed swiftly through the story of El Cid, and I was soon released.

Any surprise that Curigwen and the children may have felt at my sombre appearance soon disappeared when I presented my spoils of peace, leather coats, plates (I'm not good at fishing for trinkets) and a rapier, buttoned of course, for my son, whose pleasures were soon exhausted. My son is no D'Artagnan.

Not long home, I was summoned to a conference with Hugh 'Binkie' Beaumont, Glen Byam Shaw and Margaret Leighton. Tennent's, the leading West End management, were going to put on Ibsen's *The Lady from the Sea*. Margaret (Maggie) Leighton was to play Ellida, the lady, and they wished to see me about playing her husband, Dr Wangel. I stood beside her, and they were assured that she didn't tower over me, and we got down to talking about the play and Ibsen, about whom I knew a little to their surprise. As I sat down, I heard Maggie whisper audibly to Glen, 'Ballsy, all right!' I pretended not to notice. I had been taken aback by the subject of the conference, and my mind was just recovering.

Although Binkie was part of the Company of Four at the Lyric, Hammersmith, this was the first time that I had been asked to appear in a Tennent production. I was not their type of actor. As usual on these occasions, my mind selects the appropriate information from the layer of my library, and flashes it across my mental screen at great speed.

Binkie was a homosexual and had with his colleague, John Perry, really controlled the West End theatre between the wars, and was even now extending his policy. The policy was based on the choice of good naturalistic plays by authors like Dodie Smith, N. C. Hunter, Robert Bolt and Terence Rattigan, plays that dealt with people partially flawed – nothing like Borkman here, Ibsen's John Gabriel – in which the overall tone was one of gentle despair inviting an acceptable pity.

The language was impeccably middle-class, sufficiently laced with idiosyncratic words to invite an actor, like Richardson, say, to weave a spiral of diminishing sound to the astonished delight of his fans. The plays were always beautifully presented, by Motley sometimes. Grace abounded, it was a much sought-after commodity in a raw-boned world. The climax of playwriting in this field lay in that corner where Chekhov presided. Chekhov's plays could be treated in precisely that nostalgic manner which struck a very deep chord in the contemporary English situation. It was not so much a longing to get to a Chekhovian Moscow as to find some relief from the awful present. It was the beginning of the sixties.

To be an actor as long as I had been meant spending a great deal of my life with homosexuals, and at this moment it was in no critical mood that I looked at the present situation. Many people unacquainted with what are comically called 'queers' must wonder what sort of activities they indulge in. My concern was, now that our society was increasingly permissive there must be an increase in ethical awareness in the physical content in plays.

In Ibsen, there was a greater awareness of the subjectivity of his characters than in Chekhov. There were fewer to begin with, and while both dramatists comment on society, Chekhov's spectrum is much wider then Ibsen's, who goes deeper through sex, exploring a much greater range of sensibility. It was this that caught my attention with Eva le Gallienne's *Hedda Gabler*. The faint smell of urine which surrounds Hedda is the mark of Ibsen's irony as he explores the levels of experience she goes through in the play, with Tesman, Thea, Lövborg, Brack, until all exhausted she takes her life, hidden from all, but prompting Brack's 'People don't do such things!' Suppose Hedda, challenged by the gross sensuality of Brack, had suddenly come face to face with what must be to most women one of the most revealing aspects of herself, her frigidity? Ibsen gives no answer, but the fact that I could ascribe frigidity to Hedda's character was not only a particular view of a person in a particular situation, but a term which could be generally applied to a permissive level of society, that level occupied by sex. Was it frigidity that turned men towards their own sex? In my young days there were some actors who had, it was said, a whiff of evil about them. It was not something I could verify, but it was said that one particular actor would seize on some fresh young man, compel him to sleep with a prostitute, then rescue him for himself from the gross vulgarity of sex.

I must confess that there were no foul smells in Binkie's office when it was agreed that I would play Dr Wangel. At the time I did not know the rest of the cast but when I came to the first rehearsal my delight

53

at seeing Vanessa Redgrave, Joanna Dunham, Michael Gwynn and Richard Pasco to play the young people increased the pleasure of the prospect before me. Really, for me to play Dr Wangel now was a glorious prelude to tackling Solness and Rubek. I did not fancy *John Gabriel Borkman*, but *The Master Builder* and *When We Dead Awaken* lay before me like Himalayan peaks.

Studying the text of *The Lady from the Sea*, I was now aware of a problem that until now had been banished to the fringe of my mind. What was there about the reality and language of an Ibsen play that placed it in a different category from a play by Bolt or Rattigan, or even Shaw? Or even Chekhov, whom the English audience favoured over what they considered the doom-laden, symbolist Norwegian. Stanislavsky, whose *My Life in Art* was now necessary reading to understand the evolution through which the theatre was going, compared Ibsen's plays perversely to Chekhov's, which lay in the kitchen of life – he claimed that his company could not act the symbols, which anyway had to be repeated six hundred times to be made acceptable.

And it was not merely contemporary theatre – what of Shakespeare and the iambic pentameter that Ibsen had condemned as totally inappropriate to the new insights? And beyond Shakespeare, there lay in the Aegean islands that city-state where drama and language had been discovered. Not for the first time I cursed Rome for its cruelty and corruption that prevented the grace of Greece from permeating the rich diversity of Europe for two thousand years. The only really famous theatre in Rome was the Colosseum, a vast stadium fit for the persecution of the innocent. I could not forget that there was no theatre in Jerusalem to correct the insularity of Judaism. Judaism, that was with Roman help to provide a specious structure for the most profound insight into what it means to be an individual.

Since Ventris, much of my time had been spent on the Greek adventure, the discovery of tragedy and language, the curiosity that led men to speculate about the nature of the universe and take the first steps in the great fields of physics and biology.

Greek tragedy was the first effort to present a view of reality as a limit beyond which humanity may not go without losing its sanity. It was a limit through which the unknown comes into the lives of men as the gods share their mantle with the great heroes of the past. A total sharing that involved the death of the god in the death of the hero. If the god Agamemnon was doomed, the only language appropriate to his death was verse; only thus could the event be held where it belonged, in the past.

About this time Curigwen had seen an advertisement in *The Times* that announced that the scholars of Bradfield School were going to perform *Antigone* in the original Greek. We sat, one fine afternoon, on a stone seat, entranced as the young voices graced their way through the complex Greek metre. Sophocles was a much greater metrical innovator than Shakespeare. Later, we talked to the boy who played Antigone, who can't have been more than fourteen. After some diffidence, he explained that he didn't take Greek, that he had learned the part parrot-fashion. That he had enjoyed it, in a way.

Was there any point in looking beyond the text? If an actor, however entrancing, could learn a text automatically and repeat it without even understanding it, why should the actor be curious about the nature of his art beyond the immediacy of his performance?

The Lady from the Sea (1888) hovers between *Rosmersholm* (1886) and *Hedda Gabler* (1890). It is the last play which does not enjoy the full benefit of the technique that Ibsen had evolved for his plays: it lacks a suicide. The indirect result of this, I thought, was that Dr Wangel could not be acted with the same tormenting questions as Solness or Rubek. The play revolves round three pairs of people and 'a stranger', (John Neville). The daughters, Bolette, prepared to sacrifice happiness for security, and Hilde, the explorer of exuberance and danger in self-realization, are clear enough, and conduct their duologues accordingly with their admirers. Ellida, the Lady, is quite different. In his previous play, *Rosmersholm*, he had created in Rebecca West one of the great heroines of Scandinavian literature. So great that one of H. G. Wells's mistresses had adopted it as her pseudonym and was stuck with it.

Ellida, on the contrary, is wracked with all the wayward fantasies of dark and light, of north and south, Viking emotions. In the library of my mind there is a special shelf over which I have written the words 'The Masters of Inwardness'. The shelf contains a few works by Kierkegaard and Freud, and the plays of Ibsen. Kierkegaard's inwardness follows his insight that eternity and the historical come together as a paradox in the present moment of time. Freud's inwardness arises in his awareness that the fantasies of the mind can generate just as much power as real events. And a person so imprisoned can be liberated from them (the id) into a state of freedom when the self (the ego) can make its own choice.

I found it was in this depth of inwardness that Ibsen's new realism was revealed. And it was expressed in prose because the situation was always in the present. I saw Dr Wangel as a therapist for Ellida in her struggles with the attractions of a Stranger. The tone of the playing was quiet, and still; it was the lack of any rhetorical postures of nineteenth-century melodrama that made Ibsen's plays so difficult for the audience of his day to understand. There was no visual effort to persuade Ellida, only a deep certainty of assurance as to where her future lay. Where she would be free.

Like Shakespeare, Ibsen's growth as a dramatist extends over a long time when he was experimenting with history, time, language and form, gradually sharpening his technique until it emerges fully equipped in the prose tragedies. It is to Georg Brandes, the Danish drama critic, that we link the names of Kierkegaard and Ibsen. A Dane, he was an acute admirer of Kierkegaard, and a personal friend of Ibsen. While we can focus on the main constituents of genius like Kierkegaard or Ibsen, it was Brandes's enthusiasm to link their accidental similarity while omitting their profound insights that altered the ground of religion and tragedy. Both Kierkegaard and Ibsen believed that if reality and truth were to be appropriated in a personal sense, the communication must be indirect, allowing a maximum of freedom.

Thus Ibsen could claim that he had got rid of the monologue, meaning that he had discovered the duologue. This had appeared earlier to me in le Gallienne's *Hedda Gabler*, in Hedda's duologues with the main characters; now in *The Lady from the Sea* it was very clear that the duologue was Ibsen's main technical prop round which the characters might multiply, always returning to the two people into whom the play was focused. No Othello to say a word or two before he went, or Hamlet to predict that the rest was silence.

The magical number was two. Not merely in tragedy but in science. About this time there emerged from Cambridge University, from the work of two scientists, one of the great discoveries of a century that has been ripe in scientific discovery, the discovery of the individual.

On 2 April 1953 Francis Crick and James Watson had submitted to the scientific journal *Nature* a paper on the invariant double-helical structure of DNA, the basic constituent in the process of replication which is fundamental to life even before sex. As Bronowski put it, 'The baby is an individual from birth. The coupling of genes from both parents stirred the pool of diversity. The child inherits gifts from both parents, and chance has now combined these gifts in a new and original arrangement. The child is not a prisoner of its inheritance; it holds its inheritance as a new creation which its future actions will unfold.'

While the discovery of the significance and structure of DNA sparked

As a shepherd boy (far right) in
Oedipus Rex at Aberdeen
University, 1924.

With my sister Ivy.

At the beginning of my career.

Curigwen (above left), as Alice c1934 (above right), as Jane Eyre, 1936
(bottom left), and with George Bernard Shaw at Malvern, 1936.

With O. B. Clarence and Veronica Turleigh in the modern *Hamlet* at the Old Vic, 1938.

Roebuck Ramsden in *Man and Superman* at the Old Vic, 1939.

Our wedding, 1939. From right to left, standing: my father, Curigwen's brother Ivor Lewis (who married us), Curigwen's half-brother Dr E. A. Lewis (who gave Curigwen away), Curigwen, me, Tony Beckworth (my best man), Nancy Burman (Curigwen's best woman). Seated: Curigwen's mother (right) and my mother.

Cornwall in Granville-Barker's
King Lear at the Old Vic, 1940.
From right to left: Nicholas
Hannen, Fay Compton, me, Lewis
Casson.

Richard Burbage in *Spring 1600* at
the Lyric, 1945.

The Duke of Florence (right) in *The White Devil*, with Hugh Griffith, at the Duchess Theatre, 1947.

Family portrait, 1950. The children, from left to right: John, Marty and Harriet.

The 1950 season at the Shakespeare Memorial Theatre, Stratford-on-Avon: *Julius Caesar*, with John Gielgud (far left) and Harry Andrews (bearded).

Wolsey in *King Henry VIII*.

Leonato in *Much Ado About Nothing*, with Robert Hardy, Barbara Jefford and Peggy Ashcroft (far right).

Kent in *King Lear*, with Robert Hardy.

From the theatre programme for *Dial 'M' for Murder*, 1952.

EMRYS JONES

ANDREW CRUICKSHANK

JANE BAXTER

EY

ALAN MacNAUGHTAN

WESTMINSTER THEATRE
PALACE STREET, BUCKINGHAM PALACE ROAD, S.W.1.
(Under the Direction of The London Mask Theatre)
J. KENNETH LINDSAY
Licensed by the Lord Chamberlain to ... ... Telephone : VICTORIA 0283
Nearest Station : VICTORIA

JAMES P. SHERWOOD

presents

DIAL 'M'

FOR

MURDER

By

FREDERICK KNOTT

Nightly at 7.30 p.m.
Saturday at 5 p.m. and 8.15 p.m.
Matinee : Thursday at 2.30 p.m.

Opening Date : Thursday, 19th June, 1952

Henry Drummond in *Inherit the Wind*, at the Pembroke Theatre, Croydon, 1960.

Roebuck Ramsden in *Man and Superman* for the BBC, 1960, with James Donald and Ann Whitfield.

W. O. Gant, with Mary Ellis, in *Look Homeward, Angel*, at the Pembroke, 1960.

With Vanessa Redgrave (left) and Joanna Dunham in *The Lady from the Sea*, at Queen's Theatre, 1961.

With Sophia Loren in the film *El Cid*, 1961.

With Mary Miller in *The Master Builder*, at the Ashcroft, Croydon, 1962.

During rehearsal in the title role of *Mr Justice Duncannon*, BBC, 1963.

Dr Finlay's Casebook, BBC, 1964.
Barbara Mullen (Janet), me
(Dr Cameron) and Bill
Simpson (Dr Finlay).

With Curigwen in an early
episode of *Dr Finlay's Casebook*.

With Tom Stoppard and Wole Soyinka after the Playwright Awards, June 1967.

At Westminster Cathedral where I read the address for the Unity Service, 1968. With Cardinal Heenan, Group Captain Leonard Cheshire and Dr Horace King.

The family, 1970.

With Jack Watling and Avice Landon in *Lloyd George Knew my Father*, 1973.

With the Rt. Hon. Harold Macmillan, a fellow honorary graduate, at the Garden Party before the graduation ceremony at St Andrew's University in 1977.

Nestor at the sacking of Troy in *The Woman*, the National Theatre, 1978.

Count Orsini-Rosenberg with Simon Callow as Mozart in *Amadeus*, with the funniest line in the play: 'Too many notes, Majesty!' I had a perverse joy in tearing up a Mozart manuscript.

John Anthony in Galsworthy's *Strife*, the National Theatre, 1978.

As the lecherous abbot in *The Thrie Estaites* at the Edinburgh Festival, 1985.

A sceptical judge in Jeffrey Archer's *Beyond Reasonable Doubt*, 1987.

off an explosion in the biological sciences, its implication in the fields of politics and religion went largely by default; there having grown up in the twentieth century a superstition that science was now so complicated and arcane that only the initiated could ever hope to understand its diversity and penetrate the defences that scientists had built round themselves. The source of this attitude was the scientist's belief that the fundamental reality of the physical universe could only be expressed truly through mathematics; that the reality of, say, a Shakespeare play was only an approximation, and then only under certain conditions. I felt that the origin of this difference lay in fifth-century Athens, in the views of Plato and Socrates, as they responded to Greek tragedy. Was reality an individual acquisition of self-knowledge through an unknown god, or was it the reflection of forms elsewhere that could only be recovered by mathematics, including geometry? Of the two contrasting views, between Plato and Socrates, that of Plato was the more vulnerable, though it was given through the ages a temporal credence by the human mind's sense of its incompleteness and its tendency to attribute fulfilment to a movement elsewhere. There was always even in the Platonic universe room for God, and hence in Aristotle's sense an origin of things, a 'moving, unmoved'.

In 1958 six nations of Europe, after signing the Treaty of Rome, formed the European Economic Community (EEC). The United Kingdom was not among them. England was once again revealing its insularity. The decision would not have mattered so much had there been in the British government any awareness of a need for change. The mess that Eden had left the people in after the dismal failure of Suez did not inculcate a spirit of self-examination that should have begun with a long, hard look at the map of the world. The notion that we would survive in isolation went completely against all the facts that were looming up over the horizon.

The one dominant scientific fact that Hiroshima proved so painfully was that heaviness had surrendered to light. It was no longer necessary to assemble great batteries of guns of massive proportions to fight a war. One bomb of suitable material engineered to release a chain reaction was enough; time and light did the rest. Once the boundaries of the Koreas were set, the diverse nations of the Far East were ready to enter into competition in all those fields of commerce in which England in the nineteenth century had been supreme.

But British scientists and philosophers were much to blame; except for Eddington, few realized the potential of Rutherford's splitting of the atom, and at a time when knowledge of the universe was posing new problems of what it meant to exist, our philosophers were pursuing

57

a private enterprise, that could never be completed, about the meaning of words. It is not unexpected that one of the European thinkers who did much to mould the thought of France, Germany and Japan was the Dane Kierkegaard, whom England had rejected.

For Kierkegaard's notion of the category of the 'individual' was not exclusive; in the three spheres of existence there was always a 'Thou' as well as an 'I' – as Martin Buber saw. I was therefore enormously excited by Crick and Watson's double helix, and the uniqueness of the individual. Properly understood, it meant a total revolution in our understanding of power. It meant, for instance, an end to the Marxist concept of the dictatorship of the proletariat; the crowd was no longer the measure of value, the crowd was untruth, to belong to it meant a diminishing of the individual. It was absurd that I should feel this when the tide in England was so hostile. For it was now the beginning of the sixties, that permissive era which, in the name of freedom, thought that there was no judgement, anything goes, the group was what mattered. The flaw in this view was the inability to recognize that in any field of art or science, in politics or religion, original insights are always individual insights.

But the main loss in the growth of the crowd was the failure to realize that the search for identity, whether national or individual, had been made imperative by the new insights in society and science.

8 Another Beginning

We were moving into the sixties, and two problems loomed before me, the matter of identity, and the nature of ordinary dialogue between people. The breakdown of hierarchy, and the withdrawal of repetition as a source of self-awareness, had first been fully expressed in the nineteenth century by Wordsworth and Arnold, and was the impetus in the twentieth century for many poets like Eliot, Yeats, Lawrence and Beckett to explore the wasteland and seek for some physic to make it endurable. Something like faith or love, or, as in Beckett, an indulgence in aridity to provide a stimulus that had no real ground. 'We always find something, eh, Didi, to give us the impression we exist?' says Estragon in Beckett's *Waiting for Godot*.

My family was a great ground of reality. Curigwen's concern for them was a wonder to behold. An artist, more important than me, had she not been the theatre's ideal Jane Eyre of the century? And yet in our growth her intuition had bathed them in warmth, while from the deeps of my Scottish complexity I slowly realized that from this security I could launch my questions about identity and relationship.

To English actors it is a matter of faith that, given the talent, they must at least attempt the pinnacles of Shakespeare tragedy. It was not so with me. That I should play the leading parts in Ibsen's later plays, I now recognized, was central to my question; but there was no hurry, as the plays stretch out to old age. In the meantime I acted in what came my way, sharpening my technique of lightness and ambiguity in comedy.

I went to Vienna to make a film, *The Inspector* (USA: *Lisa*); a modest film, a thriller that made few demands. Its interest lay in the fact that

Dolores Hart, a charming young woman who was playing a leading part, had been converted to Catholicism and was to enter a convent after she'd finished the film.

When I was a very young boy in Aberdeen, an aunt of mine, born with a crooked leg that wound like a snake round the crutch that supported her when she walked, used to take me sometimes of an evening to the meeting of the local Salvation Army that gave her so much solace. Once a great evangelist was addressing the meeting. Gypsy Smith had a distrustful large moustache, but he was a powerful advocate of salvation, and at the end of the meeting he invited those who were so moved to come towards him, and confess that they were saved. Unnoticed by me, a drunk had entered the audience, and at the evangelist's invitation he jumped to his feet, and swayed down the aisle, shouting in a hoarse voice, 'Saved! Saved!' Even then it made a great impression on me. I wondered, did he know what he had done? Religion was not that easy.

I have always distrusted the immediacy of Paul's conversion; indeed I believe that after the incident on the Damascus road he withdrew into the desert to brood on what had happened to him. What, I wondered, was going on inside Miss Hart?

While in Vienna I received from my agent three episodes of a series that the BBC wished to try out. Apparently some programme had broken down, and this was to fill the gap. For years Andrew Wilson, head of the script department, had been striving to persuade them to adapt the first thirty-odd pages of A. J. Cronin's autobiography, to the point where he graduated from Glasgow University, and joined Dr Cameron. The BBC had resisted on the grounds that the commodity, with its unfamiliar language, would not be commercially viable.

Cronin had left Glasgow University in 1928, the year I left Aberdeen. Brooding on my situation, I felt vaguely a resurgence of a feeling for roots that comes from one's native land. There were three reasons why I should do the series.

I once visited an uncle in Milnathort, in Kinross-shire. He was a miner, out of work, living in one of those unyielding, granite tenements which a careless Scottish society used to spray on the wastelands surrounding our smaller cities. We were waiting for the kettle to boil in the open iron grate. The floor was wooden and bare; he sat on a horsehair sofa, an arm hanging loosely over the head. A powerful man in his shirtsleeves, his trousers were held by braces and a belt round the waist; a gold stud joined the collar of his shirt. A cigarette hung from the side of his mouth, but he showed no interest in how he smoked it. The lace curtains on the window were grey. It was a scene of memorable desolation. We had nothing to say to each other.

Again, as I looked back at my country after the First World War there were still some elements in a society that had not totally disintegrated. There were still pillars round which we could hover in relationship; pillars like the provost, the procurator-fiscal, the minister, the headmaster of the school, the doctor. It might be worth while recalling for a moment what had passed away.

But the most important consideration that seized my mind was the difference caused in our society by Sir Alexander Fleming's discovery of penicillin. I remembered how during the war army surgeons were basking in its discovery, little realizing at the time how it had opened medicine to a new microscopic dialogue as nature's imagination was stimulated to pour out inexplicable new bacteria and viruses, apparently doing naturally what was most unnatural.

Then there was the case before me, of Miss Hart, the slight indiscretion of the announcement of her conversion and intention to retreat into a convent and devote the rest of her life to the glory of God, but not yet. In due course, when she had completed the film. Conversion of any kind is a leap in understanding, but the pathos of religious conversion, particularly in Christianity, lies in the fact that it can never be seen, it is as though nothing had happened and no decision had taken place, because the religious leap consists in a new awareness of inwardness, and for this to be displayed openly would be a gross misunderstanding of the process.

In a modest way, my life was an experiment in the religious process, in my search for identity. There was first my relationship with Curigwen and the family, continually new and evolving. Then my silent brooding on Ibsen had a special and sometimes absurd place in my personal territory. Now, with the possibility of playing in a sort of scientific series on television, I could display a public face while exploring the new forces that were playing havoc with our society. Amidst the baroque windings of the pillars of St Stephen's Cathedral, I saw myself wrestling towards a new plateau of my life. I wired my agent to accept the BBC's invitation, and returned in due course to England with a bubbling but hidden excitement.

Between *The Lady from the Sea* and the film in Vienna I had played in a number of films, and made a brief appearance on television as a judge in Henry Cecil's *Brothers in Law*. The humour of this appealed to the moguls of the BBC, so that I was invited to continue the judge into a new series, *Mr Justice Duncannon*. Harry Cecil's stories were adapted for

61

television by Frank Muir and Dennis Norden, and were a delightful exercise in light comedy, as well as being a model of adaptation which *Dr Finlay's Casebook* might follow. Fortunately our first *Casebook* script editor, Harry Green, combined grace and integrity so that the series had something of an exquisite period short story without sacrificing the underlying poverty and pain of the situation, in which the doctors were ignorant of modern discoveries. With Barbara Mullen as Janet, the housekeeper, and Bill Simpson as Finlay, we were suitably differentiated.

That the series was scrambled together in haste was evident in that, for all the years (1962–9) we played in Arden House, Dr Cameron's sitting room never had a window. A conservatory, however, where he could lambast his violin with a Paganini-like ferocity, was provided. But no one seemed to notice. After the first three stories, it was very evident that the moral tone of the series had captured the early Sunday evening audience which usually goes to church. Slowly the process unfolded as the *Casebook* took its place in the production schedule of the BBC. At this time, episodes were produced in batches of thirteen, making twenty-six in a year, with a lengthy vacation during the summer. The exterior filming of the stories eventually settled in the area of Callander; otherwise production was in London studios.

The first series was almost over before I could resume the pattern of my life as I had sketched it in Vienna. Our children were growing and beginning to show the varied inclinations which signal difference. Acting in Ibsen had opened me to the levels of sensibility that exist not only in our own imaginations, but in others as our familiarity with them grows, and as they respond not merely to each other but to the experience of music, art, literature and so on. Eventually all three of them were held by the theatre, but not as artists. Only one took to acting; the others were interested in administration and technique.

Harry Green was scrupulous about the limits of medicine within which we could conduct our practice. His scrutiny of Cronin was amplified by continual reference to the *British Medical Journal* and the *Lancet* of the day. Outside the studio, a new growth was beginning to affect the young. Round the Beatles, the young were expressing a longing for something different in society that they couldn't describe with any precision. There was a paradox in that, while groups expressed their identity with the misbegotten in our society, and sang with nostalgia of the things they thought they were missing, an affluent public was paying enormous sums to share this feeling vicariously. There was nothing political in this feeling, except an ennui that could only grow, but never become a programme of revolutionary change.

My own life was becoming an immediacy after reflection, but round me I saw only immediacy without reflection.

Before the *Casebook* had settled down to its annual routine, out of the blue I was invited by Terence Kilburn to play Solness in *The Master Builder* at the Ashcroft Theatre, which had recently opened in Croydon. Mary Miller and Viola Keats were to play Hilde and Mrs Solness. It was a rush job, only two weeks for a major play to be learnt and produced. It was ridiculous. I accepted the invitation with Kierkegaardian fear and trembling, and some excitement.

When I read the play again, my reaction was very different to that of Elizabeth Robins, who confessed, 'I fear the whole thing is hopeless'. The translation was Michael Meyer's. To some, Michael's translations seem Victorian. It was precisely this which gave the actor space to breathe, where an intriguing inflection is the immediate concern. (I had by this time sorted out in my mind into what category inflections should fall, depending on the language; for descriptive verse, Shakespeare, say, the objective accent falls on what is said; for prose in Ibsen, the subjective accent falls on how it is said.)

One of Michael's salutary habits when printing his plays is to throw in extracts from critics on the original British production. It is a lesson which English critics forget too easily. The original reviews were terrible. All were inane and ignorant. Phrases like 'a feast of dull dialogue and acute dementia', 'The play is hopeless and indefensible', 'A pointless, incoherent and absolutely silly piece', 'Three acts of gibberish' abounded. It is extremely doubtful whether, in the whole history of dramatic criticism, any other major race has revealed such intellectual vapidity. However, there was Shaw and, above all, James Joyce to admire.

My mind went back to the twelve days spent with Barker on *King Lear* in 1940. Morning, afternoon and night. I was now fifty-five years old, absolutely right for the part; in the flush of life, conscious that fading was dangerously near. Rhetoric is built into the English actor's mind, precisely the quality which must be erased in acting Ibsen's prose plays. Ibsen's claim that he had got rid of the monologue was his indirect way of saying he had discovered the duologue with new depths. Two people talking, the discussion, as Shaw rationally reduced it, two people revealing themselves in wonder, surprise, despair. And the dialogue lies on the page so simply and naturally. It's only when the actor begins to 'set' the play that he becomes aware of the density of experience behind the text of the play, which is only the tip of the iceberg – and that icebergs move slowly. It's not much use here following the actor's general solution to any textual problem by 'having a dart at it'.

It is some time before Hilde appears. Then she arrives with all the impediments of a young hiker;

Hilde (goes over to Solness, her eyes alight and happy): Good evening.
Solness (looks at her uncertainly): Good evening.
Hilde (laughs): I believe you don't recognize me.
Solness: No – to be honest, just for the moment I –

Mary Miller arrived at rehearsal one day with laryngitis, her voice husky and low. Was it that husky voice, emerging as though from Cleopatra, that gave us the key to ground the play in sensuality? Words were whispered in wonder, dismay, mock pain, contradiction, it became, even in its brief period, a wonderful exercise in diction, in oral patterns that would never be complete. Even Solness's last line, when he goes off to climb the tower with the wreath given to him by Hilde, knowingly to his death, and his wife, aware that he has vertigo, tries to dissuade him;

Solness (laughing): I always do it. It is my everyday custom.

T. C. Worsley wrote of Mary Miller's performance in the *New Statesman*: 'The dangers that lie in wait for the actress playing Hilda are gush and archness. In Miss Miller's performance there is not one touch of either. The note of spontaneity is held clear and pure throughout.'

The production was well enough received for Michael Codron to transfer it to the Arts Theatre, but we ran into fogs. London's air was not then clean in winter. The season was only for a month anyway.

It was with a strange sort of relief that I returned to the *Casebook*. I had had enormous pleasure in acting Solness. It was a temporary goal in the project of my life, a minor peak that I'd climbed with many stumbling steps. Indeed, my commitment to it was such that my theatre energy was exhausted and my sensibility responded with some enthusiasm to the ailments of my patients in Scotland. My enthusiasm partly sprang from my roots in Aberdeen when I could look over the high, oyster sky of the North Sea towards Scandinavia. Ibsen was born at Skien in Norway. There was a Skene in Aberdeenshire. There had been a Ronald Skene in my class at the Aberdeen Grammar School. It was all ridiculously apt.

Indeed, as I settled down to the *Casebook* again, it was more apt than I had first thought. The message from Crick and Watson's double helix is that the individual is unique. In what sense could the individual recognize his uniqueness? Until the twentieth century the individual recognized his uniqueness in his facility to repeat the characteristics of his family, and his ability to abide by the constraints of society, and there was always an undiscovered corner of the globe to be discovered. Occasionally there were revolutions to disturb the even flow of life, but by and large knowledge and understanding were based on models inherited from the past to which everyone gave assent.

Now, however, we have been given our space. So vast that it can entertain all of us separately and spontaneously. We have been given peace; in spite of the threat of nuclear weapons, Hiroshima ensured that. This really was Einstein's world that we were being forced to understand. Whereas Newton's world was dominated by a fundamental heaviness in which everything could be adjusted, and measured, now lightness prevailed everywhere. To Democritus in fifth-century Athens, there was ultimately only atoms and the void. Now even the void existed as a mass of fields of interpenetrating waves and particles that were invisible and weightless. I was suddenly very tired, then I giggled. It was really absurd for an actor to think he could do anything about it. Yet somehow I couldn't stop. I must be prepared to make a fool of myself.

I think what first attracted me to Sir Charles Sherrington, the great physiologist, and excited me enormously was his amazing description of the eye. This occurs in his collection of the Gifford lectures he gave at the age of eighty in Edinburgh in 1937–8 and published in 1940, *Man on his Nature*.

That was the year when as Cornwall I had gouged out Gloucester's eyes in Barker's *King Lear*. It was also the year when some children playing at Lascaux discovered the cave whose wall was covered with a perfect drawing of a horse, which French archaeologists tell us was executed some ten thousand years ago, a leap that was the first real proof that man's mind, memory and imagination were very young.

We had not taken account of these things because halfway through the year Hitler's tanks penetrated the Maginot line, and our very existence was threatened – in glorious weather. Only now did my memory restore them to my mind. Indeed, was there something in playing Cameron in the *Casebook* on television, living simultaneously in two years, 1964 and 1930, that stimulated my imagination to reflect on my identity in an unusual, scientific way? The memory creates the self, but the memory only retains what has been experienced through the mind. The imagination knits the external world into the fabric of the mind, thus completing the molecule or field in the brain. So it is through the imagination that the mind is suddenly invaded from the unconscious. The intrusion is accelerated and experienced in the present, because only the mind is now.

The new series of the *Casebook* was going well, my reading in science extending indiscriminately between physics and biology. But I was able to hold them apart, no question of equivalences.

A lesson I had learnt in talking with physiologists was not to confuse my sense of reality with theirs. There was therefore in my reading no urge to see equivalences between the wave/particle ground of quantum mechanics and the protein/nucleic acid of biology, although they both shared the number two. But I was already aware of the situation. Thus Milman Parry can describe the *Iliad* as conjuring an analogy, a kind of likeness to the society of the Trojan world, so helping us to understand it. But Clerk Maxwell's equations were not an analogy of Faraday's electromagnetic fields, though he uses the word frequently in response to Faraday's plea to put his equations into words that he can understand. As a Scotsman, I was greatly drawn to Clerk Maxwell, arguably the greatest scientist between Newton and Einstein.

Halfway through the spring of 1964, I was invited to a Sunday night reading of a play adapted by Felicity Douglas and Basil Dawson from a novel of Harry Cecil, *Alibi for a Judge*. It was very funny and I promised I would do it after the present batch of the *Casebook* was over.

In due course, towards the beginning of summer the batch of the *Casebook* was completed, and I began rehearsing *Alibi*. The idea was to open at the Grand Theatre, Leeds, for the beginning of a four-week tour, then consider the future in view of all my commitments. Hugh Goldie was directing, and the play rehearsed well. After the first night, it was clear that the play had possibilities. The audience laughed a great deal.

Curigwen came up on the Wednesday to see the play. It was 12 August, grouse shooting day; the day on which we'd been married in 1939. The day and the play were two things to celebrate.

In 1939, grouse shooting day, a Saturday, dawned beautifully, the sun showing a warm interest in the parish church of Evencoed, peering silently at the gentle Radnorshire moors that surrounded it. Curigwen had spent the previous night in the vicarage, I in a hotel at Presteigne close by. In the morning, we joined up and were married by her brother, Ivor.

We had to return immediately to London as I was in the middle of rehearsals at the Old Vic for the second Buxton Festival. We had arranged to spend the night at the Mitre Hotel, in Oxford. Two friends of Curigwen's, the poet Louis MacNiece and the German lecturer

Ludwig Stahl, were giving us a party; a future radio producer R. D. Smith and the novelist Olivia Manning, who married around the same time, were at the party; and so was one who, unnoticed by me at the time, was to prove immediately relevant to the direction in which my thoughts were moving after the war, Professor E. R. Dodds, author of *The Greeks and the Irrational*. In the nineteenth century, there had grown up through Goldsworthy Lowes Dickinson and others an image of the Greeks as detached, controlled, grave senators, blessed with enormous gifts of organizing things rationally. Dodds altered all that. I now see them as radical and volatile, of great reflection and energy.

Curigwen saw the play, and on Thursday, the next day, she returned to London – we had three growing children. That night, when I had gone to bed, something happened. Normally we do not question what our body does. Beneath our skin there is an extraordinary mechanism which seems to conduct an experiment with life all by itself. We are told of needs that have to be satisfied in order that we might conduct our enterprises, but that does not really explain the amazing simultaneity with which the body works, for it is always in the present. The 'now' of the mind is the 'now' of the body. Both are in the present, neither in the past, nor the future. Again, when we go to bed, the body seems glad to settle down to the rest.

Suddenly I found myself staring at the ceiling. Something was going on inside me. I walked over to the washbasin to pee. Nothing! Well, a drop or two. Nothing like the great flush that my mind told me was necessary to liberate me from the pain that was busily thrashing my stomach. It was after twelve. I phoned down to the hotel's reception and was more or less told that unless I was at death's door, nothing could be done until morning. I should have yelled at them; but I understand people too well, and I sympathize with their reluctance to help me.

It had not been so in Manchester with Donat. Then I had terrified my landlady with my voice into summoning the doctor after midnight; he took one look at me with my arm over the bedhead and whisked me into Withington Hospital. That time I might have died of delay. A perforated ulcer poisons! Would it happen this time? Had anyone died of an inability to pee? Of course not. It was ridiculous. I laughed and sidled over to the washbasin. Nothing again.

By the time it reached one o'clock, and I had fruitlessly visited the washbasin at least a dozen times, I came to the conclusion that I was not going to die. Nature had said to herself that she was going so far in this man's body and no further. This restraint of nature engendered a warm response in my mind, and as usual on these occasions I began to brood on the human condition, or more accurately myself. I thought of Democritus of fifth-century Athens, in somewhat similar circumstances conducting a dialogue between his mind and his senses. I had by now settled into a prone posture on my back, staring at the ceiling. Outside, the night was warm and quiet. My mind was having an argument with my body. 'Obviously,' I was saying, 'there is colour, some sweetness, some bitterness and' (this with some feeling) 'clearly pain, actually' (very wryly) 'only atoms and the void.' I paused. There was something wrong here. Democritus goes on to say that the senses provided the evidence for the mind, and what the mind might think in its superior way is a victory, is really a defeat. I paused again. Time was passing. It was now two o'clock and my visits to the washbasin were passing in an automatic haze.

In a weak voice with little conviction I murmured, 'Physician, cure thyself.' The androgens were leaping about in my prostate gland like Maxwell's demons, and I could do nothing about them except respond painfully to their agitation. But when was I responding – at the same time or later? Democritus had thought that space was empty, Hiroshima had taught us that space was not empty; that fields of great power interpenetrated the universe in all directions, fields of power that were weightless and invisible. Did they penetrate the eye?

Did light penetrate the eye and thus accelerate the sluggish impulses of the nervous system into the present moment of time? If it were like this, then the mind could be said to be the point of control for the memory and the imagination. One thing was certain, I would remember this, and as to my imagnation I knew that I was no poet, and would never celebrate the passing of this night in verse, which I suppose is a kind of proof of my imagination – as Keats would say, of negative capability. I paused.

It was getting on for four o'clock, and the August sun was beginning to creep around the room. Such is the speed with which the body adapts to circumstances that my modest pilgrimage to the washbasin had become a ritual, and that the desired fruits should be forbidden was anticipated. But I persevered.

Seven o'clock. One last tentative exploration to show that my urge to live had not drained away entirely. But there was no new revelation. I reached for the telephone, and asked the porter to come and see me, and bring a pot of tea.

Now that I had a witness, things moved quickly. Dr Raper arrived about nine. The diagnosis was swift. The sickness obvious. He was a gracious man and, fortunately, a urologist of note. Curigwen was informed. The second time my frail body had vented its vulnerability on her like a bolt from the blue. And, of course, the management.

We yapped for a time, and as clearly I was not prone, it was decided (agreed reluctantly by Dr Raper) that I should play that Friday night, and then go into the Brotherton Wing of Leeds General Hospital on Saturday for an operation to be arranged as soon as possible.

For the performance, a bucket was to be placed at either side of the stage in case a miracle might happen. It was really astonishing how I got through the performance that night, not because of the pain that I was going through, but because of the thought of these buckets waiting expectantly. I missed the two performances on Saturday, much to the chagrin of my understudy, who had not learned the part. He had to go on and read it. I had much sympathy with him. We had both been caught short.

Getting into hospital was a relief. I was in some pain that was relieved when I received a catheter which at least restored a trickle of my babbling brook. I could walk about with it – rather slowly, like a Roman senator enjoying the baths at Pompeii. What it did was to transform the urge to live, which I share with all human beings, into a precise and personal will to live.

In the afternoon I go to bed. A delicious nurse (all nurses are delicious) asks me if I'm comfortable. I look at her incredulously. If I were truly uncomfortable I'd be screeching my guts out. I am an actor I know how to scream. Instead, I smile and thank her for her interest. To myself I say, 'Job went through worse'.

It was early evening in August. There were no football crowds outside to disturb the beating peace of this Saturday night. Hume, the Scottish philosopher, was right about the discontinuity of impressions that invade the mind, and Freud was right about a place in the mind called the subconscious. My mind was open to impressions from anywhere.

The light filtering into the ward reminded me of a night in Aberdeen when I was a very young boy, about seven. We had only three rooms in our tenement flat; no bathroom, an outside loo four floors down. I slept in the front parlour, nightly turned into my bedroom, on the couch. The light from the gas lamplights below fixed on the ceiling above me. Some drunks passed up the street outside, in that condition that chimes easily with God. They were singing, 'O, for a closer walk with God/A calm and sweet repose'.

Years later, when I was a young actor playing in a thriller, *The Silent Witness* by Jack de Leon, some idiot had booked the company to play in Cork – during Lent. On Good Friday, I dropped into a Catholic Church. I listened with a fascinated horror to the priest's sermon that was determined to make God's judgement a most terrifying thing, a brew familiar in Scotland – but here? Of course! Now I recognized it. It was the Easter Sermon that James Joyce had pinned down in *Portrait of the Artist as a Young Man*. Our backgrounds in some respects were very similar.

I was beginning to sweat, and thought I should keep still for a moment. I was thirsty, orange and grapefruit waters were at hand, provided under the name Robinson. I drank and gloated over the deserts of Arabia where thirst is a contingency of life.

It was getting dark, and the nurse was hovering about me. I was still in some pain, but when I looked at the haggard creatures that surrounded me, my pain could be endured. It was a funny pain. I'd not been wounded in battle, no Irishman had spewed his bile on me; no student had poured his contempt on me. My own body had expressed its anger. One part had exploded on another, and my mind could do nothing about it except endure, in patience.

'Do you want to go to sleep?' It was the nurse talking; they are very attractive, these nurses who ask such questions. 'In a little,' I said. 'I'll bring you something,' she said, and she left me. I was glad. I had a feeling Freud was getting at me.

The nurse, that delicious creature with the nipped-in waist that beckoned me, was playing about with some bottles in the corner of the ward. Totally oblivious, she did not know I was in the process of seducing her. And, such is the speed of the mind on these occasions, I'd gone through the whole rigmarole of dragging her under my sheets, my catheter abandoned, touched her breasts with beautiful Greek detachment, and then the slow leisurely indulgence of love as practised by two civilized creatures who know precisely what they are doing, how to measure their love and get the maximum satisfaction out of the sexual act; and then (here I caught myself smiling) are mature enough to have no sense of guilt about it. It was all over in a trice. The creature above me was smiling. I lay inert, emptily staring at her. 'Something to make you sleep,' she said. I swallowed the pill, with a gulp of water. I just heard my voice say, 'Thank you.' I had a feeling it was very weak, and not a bit like Don Giovanni's.

I slept well, and woke early on the Sunday. How was I to get through the day? The operation was not due to take place until 2.30 on Monday afternoon, by which time Curigwen would be here. Curigwen! Shaw called her the girl with the unpronounceable name.

Up till now events had imposed an immediacy on my thought that had deprived me from considering the consequences of the operation that I was to have on the Monday. A world of women in which I was impotent? An empty, cold place? There really were only two women in my life, and I had been married to both.

In 1933, I took part in a tour of some of the small towns in the West Country in a play by E. M. Delafield, *To See Ourselves*. Playing opposite me was a blonde girl with a slow, deep voice. Her name was Stella Wynyate. It was a stage name. Her real name was Stella Constance Bickerton, and her father was a well-known eye specialist. She had taken the name from Compton Wynyates, a place she loved. We fell very much in love, and set up house together when we returned to London. Late that year I played in a musical comedy, *Command Performance*, understudying Dennis King. (I got my first job in Shakespeare playing Feste in *Twelfth Night* and Amiens in *As You Like it* because I could sing.) King, an Englishman, had made his reputation in America in musicals like *The Vagabond King* (filmed 1930) and *The Three Musketeers*, and had quite legitimate pretensions to acting. While in London, with Bill Mollison he had bought the American rights of *Richard of Bordeaux*. He intended to act in it in New York in the spring of 1934. He asked me to play Maudleyn, Richard's page in the play, a very sympathetic part.

Stella and I decided to get married; and to avoid all the problems of an English wedding, we arranged to be married on the American liner *United States* on our way to New York.

On arrival in New York we stayed at the Algonquin just long enough to see the actor Ernest Milton and the critic Alexander Woollcott having breakfast together on a Sunday morning, before we moved out to the Barbizon Plaza, which was much less expensive. It was also closer to West 57th Street and Carnegie Hall, which was to provide, at least musically, one of the most vivid experiences in my life.

The play rehearsed well with a distinguished cast that included Montague Love, an English actor long resident in Hollywood. Coming to New York, he decided to deposit his money in the Bank of the United States, and lost it all in the Crash. Francis Lister and Margaret Vines had come from England. We had something like five weeks of rehearsal before opening at the Colonial Theatre, Boston. Our life was full of stillness and discovery. Everything was familiar and different. The mathematician and philosopher A. N. Whitehead was at that time a resident professor at Harvard. Stella admired his collaborator, Bertrand Russell, but he was too clever for me.

Spring was beginning when we returned to New York; the air from Central Park was like champagne. It did not matter that the play was not a great success – King had not quite made the transition. One day after a matinee I found a note from Stella at the stage door. It read 'Darling. Je suis enceinte, love S.'

71

At that time the New York Philharmonic Orchestra used to give their concerts on Thursday evenings, and, such was the support for the orchestra, repeat the same programme on Friday afternoons. We had been introduced to Miriam Berlow of Steinway's, and in her gentle American concern for two poor English actors, she thought it might sustain us to attend the Friday afternoon concerts. Thanks to her generosity, we heard the complete cycle of Beethoven symphonies that Toscanini used to conduct every spring with the orchestra, together with the various concertos. The season always ended with Verdi's Requiem, which we also caught. A grace had descended on our lives, that would live for ever.

An MGM scout, Billy Grady, arranged a film test for me but it was not successful. The weather was improving; and just before it became intolerable, the play came off, and we set out for five weeks on a short tour to Washington, Pittsburgh and Chicago. In Washington it was cherry blossom time, and we explored ourselves through visits to Mount Vernon, George Washington's place, and leisurely days on the banks of the Potomac, reading the biography of the great Russian ballet dancer Vaclav Nijinsky which had just been published. Pittsburgh passed unmemorably, and so to Chicago.

We had a small apartment in a block just off Grand Avenue, leading to Lake Michigan. Up to now, we had been living in hotels, and though Stella was getting larger as her pregnancy became more obvious, the domestic chores were not exhausting. Then events overwhelmed me with a numbing rapidity. The tour ended. The 1934 World Fair was about to open in Chicago, containing an English Village, the centrepiece of which was a replica of the Globe Theatre, in which potted versions of Shakespeare's plays were performed. I was approached to play King Hal.

Stella became ill. A great fog had descended on Chicago. The topsoil from the farms of the Midwest had been blown off by the wind, and the city had been transformed into a sort of perpetual night. Stella's left ear was infected, and her head was covered in bandages. Dr Fitzpatrick, a kindly American doctor, eventually decided she must be moved into the Henrotin Hospital, where she died a fortnight later of a meningeal virus. My colleagues were very understanding. Stella was cremated in Chicago with her unborn child. I took her home to England, to rest in Steyning, Sussex, a place that had known our love.

Haunted by these memories of thirty years before, I moaned in my bed, and tried to wriggle but movement was limited. The afternoon was drawing on quietly. I struggled out of my bed, and crossed to the window of the ward, high in the hospital, overlooking the Leeds City

Hall. They held competitions for young pianists here, individuals testing their skills. Soon I would have to test my skill – with a diminished body, except that my negative capability was directing my thoughts towards the two women in my life. So different, yet each providing a partial model of the levels on which people live their lives, at least according to Ibsen.

Sunday, 16 August 1964 was the time when the mosaic of my life began to materialize as points in my identity. I saw the history of my art as growing out of the insights, technique and energy of the men and women who lived in Athens and the islands of the Aegean, at least five centuries before Christ. They had provided the model for Shakespeare and the Elizabethan world, and a pattern for Ibsen and the twentieth century. I must hold on to this, for it was thus that my art, such as it was, took its place in our society.

The great expanse of Europe extended over me, and in the middle of this great hospital I was alone. I shuddered. There mounted within me a great anger and fear of the crowd. For years before the war the 'Sieg Heil's of Nuremberg had stunned our minds, and stricken our wills. Mercifully, we had survived. The crowd was untruth.

In striving to find a truthful relationship with two women, I had learnt much about myself. Curigwen was immediate, spontaneous, open and light; Stella was grave, reflective and considered. Between them they had provided me with the immediate experience of those layers of sensibility whose exploring brought me such richness. They were the layers that I sought to discover in Ibsen. For if art is the solution to problems that cannot be solved in any other way, then the theatre was surely fitted to explore those fields of inwardness which are the unique possession of every individual.

The nurse came to quieten my uneasy body. Before I took the pill, I stared at her straight in the eye and smiled, 'Hume was wrong; there is a purpose in life. Two people listening to each other in silence. An artist saying something to me in words thousands of years old. It's a sin to describe them. It's all a mystery.' I took the pill, and sipped from the glass. She nodded. I hope she understood.

When I had had my operation, Curigwen with her immediate desire for truth insisted that she be told everything, and my surgeon, Mr Raper, assured her that there was nothing malignant. This was very consoling, since almost everyone assumed that such an operation concealed an evil growth, such was the universal fear of cancer.

General de Gaulle had been operated on for a prostate reluctance; so had Harold Macmillan, and an American pop singer, Frankie Laine. I was told it was very fashionable, and I was in good company, something I appreciated only partially.

After the operation, they moved me into a private room, which stimulated me to even greater reflection on myself and my new condition. I realized that the management of the play must have lost some money on it, and I promised to do it in 1965 in my next break from the *Casebook*. Curigwen returned home to the family who had sent me their love. I was now alone in Leeds. But assured of work for a considerable time.

Ever since Barker's *King Lear* of 1940, when he had spelt out the measurements of the play, I had with a kind of instinct applied his principles to my own life. It was a series of equations, of weights and balances, as I measured the various elements of my life in terms of fulfilment, so approaching some understanding of the kind of reality that it was now possible for an individual to achieve. My mind and body, my family, my work, the society in which I lived, its history and place in the new world of light, for I was now assured that light permeated every aspect of existence. Einstein had replaced Newton, gravity, heaviness, had been replaced by light, which was the source of a continual acceleration. Wondering whether I could contribute anything to the problem of mind, which the neurophysicists were trying to fix, or rather the problem of mind, memory and imagination, as I saw it. 'As I saw it' – when I said this, I couldn't help laughing. It was ridiculous. I was an actor, and the English don't trust actors except when they are on the stage.

My solution was to turn to Kierkegaard. This was fairly safe, since the English knew nothing of Kierkegaard, and it would be a further step along the road in the task I had set myself. Just as he asked himself how he could go beyond Socrates, so I asked myself how I could go beyond Kierkegaard. It was all absurd, but it was the start of a pattern.

Kierkegaard was twenty-eight when he jilted his fiancée, Regina Olsen, in October 1841; later in October, he left for the University of Berlin, where he entered the Philosophy class under Professor Friedrich Schelling, who had just suceeded to the chair once occupied by G. W. F. Hegel. In his class were Friedrich Engels (the future collaborator of Marx), Mikhail Bakunin, and the anarchist Max Stirner, who later was to compose the classic work on anarchism. In May 1842 Kierkegaard returned to Copenhagen, complaining to his brother Peter that Schelling 'drivelled on'.

He returned to Berlin three times between 1842 and 1855, the year of his death. In these thirteen years he had produced the most profound analysis of religious experience since St Paul, and had laid (so I thought) the foundations for a new dispensation of society. Of the various circumstances that combined to produce his behaviour, two meant much to me: his introspection, and his acute sense of time. I could not share in the desolation of his inwardness which produced so many new insights, but his sense of time I shared deeply. In my profession, my experience of the past in the plays of Aeschylus and Shakespeare, up to the near-present of Ibsen had shaped the growth of my mind and body as an actor. I had learned the use of language in poetry as descriptive and objective, or in prose to be inflected ambiguously and inward. As to time, his sense of the present anticipates the 'now' of Einstein and Max Planck, the quantum theorist. To me, time and light are identical.

So, in one sense, I would leave Leeds General Hospital and return to London, much as Kierkegaard returned to Copenhagen, with one kind of work before me. But I had one advantage over him. As a springboard, he had only reflections on his father, whereas I had a wife and family entire, without any danger of its being extended.

9 Callander

When I got out of hospital, Curigwen and I left for Scotland by way of recuperation and to find a place to stay during the next batch of the *Casebook*. The Roman Camp hotel at Callander was I think closing for the winter. After a time wandering round the countryside, we found the Lake Hotel, settled low on the banks of the Lake of Menteith. The only (lake as distinct from loch) in Scotland, it held an island at its centre on which rested the ruins of Inchmaholme Castle, where Mary, Queen of Scots, had been incarcerated for a time on her way to further imprisonment in England. The hills round the lake were low and irregular. The sky very high. Peace sits on this place, much of the kind that Yeats found on Innisfree.

The hotel had just been taken over by Davy Nisbet, a publican from Stirling, and his wife, a frail, pale woman, always dressed in black, who drifted inconsequently about the hotel, as though she were looking for somewhere else. She suffered permanently from shingles that never improved. The hotel was really run by his son Bobby, an overt teetotaller, and Elma, Bobby's diligent wife.

They were uncertain as to whether to close for the winter but it was so obviously appropriate for our purpose that with Campbell Logan, our producer, we persuaded them to remain open for the company.

We returned to London greatly refreshed. The children were growing, beginning to explore Europe. The movement towards 'the instant' was gathering pace. The volatility of the universe and the irrational in human behaviour that was implicit in the equation of Einstein, a Jew, had never been faced and analysed. The solution had been to abandon history, and concentrate on the instant, the now of

76

experience, without reflection. My reading of Sherrington had by now persuaded me to dwell on the mind, the memory and the imagination. The advances that Sherrington himself had made – he had discovered the synapses in the nervous system – had brought us to the boundaries of science as far as the mind was concerned. I now thought that the way forward was to be found in a synthesis of some kind between the whole body and the artefacts it created (that is, its art).

The new wholeness of man, men and women seen as subjects, the phenomenon of the twentieth century, I felt in the new question that artists should now be asking about the universe and the nature of life. To observe the magnitude of the heavens, to sense the great diversity of humanity that was spawned upon the earth – and in my bewilderment to ask 'Why?' – was to be stricken by a paralysis. But to feel the harmony of all things and beings at one moment of time was to recover my wonder and whisper 'How?' The great shifts in understanding are basically very simple. We had not yet learned to ask the new question 'How?' Darwin and Freud were fearful at the discoveries they were making about nature and life, precisely because they felt that the new questions would never be asked.

In the sixties, the movement in my own profession, and indeed over the body social, was towards entertainment. The nature of the new reality was never questioned. Value and truth were abandoned as impediments to the new discovery of permissiveness which brought instant fulfilment. For permissiveness was confused with openness, a very different thing.

I would not have experienced this so vividly had I not felt so distinctly in my own person the divide between mind and body; we were still dominated by a variety of Cartesianism. Now that I was truly divided between my mind and my body, any movement towards wholeness must come from the mind. The notion of 'holism' had really started with the South African soldier/politician Jan Smuts but it had been given a medical orientation. The great quest of neurophysiologists was to locate that part of the brain in which the mind worked. My feeling at this time was that even if the scientist *did* discover some cell or organ in the brain traceable to the mind, the discovery could not account for the individual workings of the memory and the imagination. The uniqueness of man's mind, as proved by the prehistoric drawings at Lascaux and Altamira, was that it did not evolve but was a leap. Hence the amazing wholeness and maturity of the drawings, compared with the primitive nature of the scratchings and agriculture which preceded them. The mind of the artist at Lascaux was very similar to my own. It was the environment that changed.

When I returned to England from the USA in 1935, my first work was at the Gate Theatre in Villiers Street, run by a Scotsman, Norman Marshall. Two of the plays in which I appeared at that time loomed before me now. I played Karl in *Karl and Anna*, a German play by Leonhard Frank. During the First World War, Karl had spent a long time in the trenches with a brother soldier who went into great detail about his wife and their life together, so that when his friend was killed Karl felt he knew so much about their domestic life that he decided to take the place of his friend; the wife was Anna. It was a great illumination of a schizophrenic imagination.

The second play that affected me at this time was *Oscar Wilde*. Robert Morley played Wilde, his first part of substance; Mark Dignam was the prosecuting counsel, Carson; I played Clark, for the defence. The play focused in a most immediate sense what must always remain for the homosexual the spiritual problem: was Wilde's sensibility of love so expansive as to bring his practice of masturbation and sodomy with a pretty stable-boy into harmony with the depth of his mind?

The immediacy of pleasurable sensation that can be achieved in any sexual experience creates a desire for its repetition; but such repetition is only fulfilling when it is accompanied by a kind of loving which brings in the mind. When mind is not present, sexual pleasure becomes a promiscuous exercise for the body. It is usually detectable by the eye. J. R. Ackerley, a flower of the BBC, tells of a journey to Scotland, when, having lunch on the train, he caught the eye of one of the waiters, and withdrew with £5 to the cramped quarters of the carriage lavatory to enjoy an erotic toss or two.

During the autumn and winter of 1964 the *Casebook* continued, and I grew stronger. A programme began to form in my mind, though like all existential projects it had jagged edges. But then all existential thinking is concerned with the now of the self, the discovery of what inwardness means.

The influence of Barker had been fruitful in organizing myself in relation to the external world of experience and life. Now the life and notions of Simone Weil, a Catholic religious thinker of Jewish origin, fascinated me. Born a year or so after me in Paris, she died in Ashford, Kent in 1943, aged thirty-four. The stages of her life were marked out by a mixture of design and providence. She admired Kierkegaard less than me, but our love of the Greeks was a mutual passion, and we both sought knowledge. But the single element in her thought which I shared was a peculiar understanding of the intensity of suffering which is the source of inward passion.

In the decades immediately after the war, the BBC's Third Programme (later Radio 3) was arguably the greatest source of a new knowledge in England. Oppenheimer, Herbert Butterfield and others threw a new light on the great range of sciences that the discoveries of Darwin and Einstein had released. In religion, there was a new urgency about biblical studies, and great speculation about the historical Jesus. Somewhere along the line John Robinson, an Anglican bishop, had affronted the faithful with an attempt to be *Honest to God*. But it was very dim theology compared to the dry intensity of a Simone Weil or John of the Cross. I turned to the Continent, to the defeated nations for the new theology. To Bultmann and Buber, Tillich and Jaspers, but not uncritically, for I was finding that my absorption with Ventris and his decipherment was opening up for me a completely new understanding of the classical world. A thought kept pounding through my mind: there was no theatre in Jerusalem. And again, there is no separation between the classical and modern world. Civilization is a thread that stretches out in one line from Lascaux to all the world.

The notion of one world of civilization had to be held in the mind together with the infinite diversity of its revelation. Thus I found Simone Weil's last words some consolation in the direction I was moving. The last sentence she is believed to have written is: 'The most important part of education – to teach the meaning of to *know* (in the scientific sense).' The implication I read into this was that knowledge for the artist must be balanced and corrected by the fundamentals of science, and vice versa, that the scientist in his empirical limits must be aware of the paradox of the unknown.

Out of these currents there might emerge a style of living. I was acutely aware of this. Acting in the *Casebook* with its somewhat jejune views of science of the early years of the century, and as looming before me Christmas approached, the problem of fitting in the vulnerability of a Judge, my acting life was balanced as it had been for years on the moral dilemmas of professional people, for I had never in my career played an ordinary man.

My Christmas gift from Curigwen was, as usual, a year's subscription to the London Library in St James's Square. Before the war, I had studied in the British Museum Reading Room. But now, to take books home, what a pleasure!

The initial problem for me in 1965 was one of work, the *Casebook* and

Alibi for a Judge; how to fit them in, if at all possible. Normally, actors in a series wait until it is completed before they engage in a further run. The decision then depends on the TV organization, which decides by a complex process of calculation whether to continue or cut. But both the *Casebook* and *Alibi* were what is called in the profession proved propositions. I explained my dilemma about *Alibi* to the BBC. They were very understanding. It was decided that when the *Casebook* finished round April, I could start the play. If it ran, and a new series of the *Casebook* happened in the autumn, they would write me out of all locations (which were now being organized in Scotland from the Lake Hotel), and record the series at the Riverside Studios, Hammersmith (later an Arts Centre) on Sundays and Mondays, ensuring that recordings on the Monday would finish in time for me to get to the theatre.

Much to my surprise, and I think everyone else's, this is exactly how it happened. In the autumn, I found myself working every night of the week. By way of diversion I turned to theology. The play, *Alibi for a Judge*, was produced at the Savoy Theatre and ran for twenty months.

I had made my first professional appearance in London at the Savoy Theatre in the summer of 1930, after eighteen months in the provinces. The play was *Othello*, with Paul Robeson, Peggy Ashcroft and Maurice Browne. Browne had made an enormous amount of money out of a production of R. C. Sherriff's *Journey's End*, which he had picked up from a try-out at the Arts Theatre. At one time there were about six companies touring the play in Britain. This was just before what was called the 'talkies' came in to put an end to such vulgarity. He was an Englishman who'd been caught up in the Chicago Little Theatre, and it was from there that Ellen Van Volkenberg came to direct *Othello*. I walked on and such was American thoroughness that I became third understudy to, I think, Cassio.

Apart from Robeson's playing of Othello, which was extremely athletic and movingly tender, there were few things to note about the time: a party for Peggy Ashcroft, then recently engaged to the future publisher Rupert Hart-Davis; the sets of James Pryde; the costumes of John Armstrong. Pryde was one half of the artists known as the Beggar-staff Brothers, who had designed sets for the Lyceum – the other half was Albert Rutherston. My most vivid recollection of the play is of Robeson's dresser, a black West Indian, Andrews by name. He was an excellent cricketer, and one of his duties was to ply Robeson with champagne, so that in our warm summer by the end of the play when Othello is to make his last entrance in his woollen nightwear, and I was close to him, the indescribable odour of mothy champagne and perspiration descended on me. Quite unforgettable.

As this somewhat tangled routine of television and theatre continued into the autumn of 1965, I found my own position within it intriguing, in that it prompted a scrutiny of my memory as it was used in the theatre in the evening, and learning the *Casebook* scripts by day. Taken with the casual ideas and notions that appeared, uninvited, in my mind, I was on the way to evolving a practice of system controls for my mind, memory and imagination. The Greeks discovered this practice, now aptly called by the Greek-derived name, cybernetics. They recognized the irrational in life, which would overwhelm them unless subjected to some kind of control. They invented a saying to deal with it: 'Nothing too much.' I saw it as a limit. Greek tragedy was a limit beyond which travel was forbidden; otherwise the furies would get you.

It amused Peter Naylor, the actor's chaplain at the Savoy, to come into my dressing-room during an interval and find me reading Bultmann's *Theology of the New Testament*. I said there was no accounting for taste, but I read theology as other people read Agatha Christie – I found it fun. There was, however, another and perhaps deeper reason which I did not go into. Indeed, how could I ever explain to him what Ventris meant to me? For I was by now convinced that the implications of his cracking the Linear B text into its vowel, consonant and syllable elements was the foundation of the tremendous superiority of Greek civilization over others of the time, and the necessary ground for all the art and science that followed it – communication, diction, was born.

Nagging at my mind was the total failure of the Established Church, or indeed any religion, to understand what science was about. The excuse that was continually offered was that religion was not of this world. I found this to be a lie, manufactured by jealous civil servants to maintain their power through fear and superstition. And yet, and yet, I could not explain why I was finding my explorations into the foundations of religion so satisfying. Because it was not as though I found my questions answered, but rather that one thing led to another, and I found the inquiry deeply satisfying, and continually inviting because never finished.

Yet, when I settled down to Bultmann's *Theology* I was faced with a familiar problem. Just after the war I'd tried to read Darwin's *The Origin of Species*, and had got no distance in it before recognizing that it was entering fields of particularity into which I was forbidden. I did not think that my mind was incapable of facing such specialization, but rather that I had misunderstood the nature of evolution. The notions of movement and change must be held together, as the fundamentals on which the whole universe exists, since these notions subsist in every mode of life. Evolution is the one word which embraces this process. Yet evolution reveals itself in every element as essentially simple. (J. Bronowski suggests that the magical number in mathematics is two.) But given the essential simplicity of evolution and its self-generating genius for discovering new elements, once these are vivid, their capacity and pace to proliferate into an unsuspected diversity was staggering.

Ventris, my reading of Greek history, my familiarity with Greek tragedy, had set up ideas about society. Societies grew and declined, I thought, according to a basic process which I saw as an interpenetration of insights, technique, and energy. Thus fifth-century Athens was the model of this molecule of creation for the whole range of activities we know as the process of life. Again, when I looked at the Jews I thought that first-century Palestine before the birth of Christ represented the model for civilization of a race and a family held in the gathered text of the Old Testament. The New Testament was about the individual. It was possible to see the genealogy quoted by Matthew at the beginning of his Gospel as marking Jesus within a continuing Jewish tradition. It was also possible to see the story of the virgin birth as a discontinuity, a break with tradition. Biblical criticism was raising all sorts of questions without disturbing the basic kernel of faith.

With Paul, we see the first leap towards God as a concept without which a man cannot achieve identity and authenticity, the ground being man's awareness of self in its double presence as body and mind. Paul was the great advocate of Hellenistic Christianity. It was with some distress that I recognized this, since all the movement in the Church today was towards taking on board a burden of Judaistic ballast that prevented the buoyancy of belief.

It was while I was brooding on this that I wondered whether my performance in the play was being affected by the dialogue going on in my mind. The timing of a play's performance is always measured against the timing of the first performance. So now I used to go to the prompt corner after every act to check the time. Strangely, there was no lengthening – I was told once of a successful play that had put on seventeen minutes' playing time in a year. Such is the self-indulgence of actors before a captive audience. But what other profession was so sensitive to internal and external pressures?

When I am sent a play to read with a view to playing in it, the text is the sole guide as to how I understand the play and my part in it. This is not how I read the Bible, which I do not hold to be infallible. The Bible is a text of its time and times, having a history of language and customs behind it, having a situation and a mixed bag of people to carry on its actions which may be good or evil. But when I came to read the New Testament closely, I was so held by the vitality and clarity of the authors' imaginations that my critical functions were stretched to a higher sensitivity to detect omissions and non-sequiturs. For instance, the two massive omissions in Paul which caused continual wonder were his neglect of the Virgin Birth, and his failure to see that the last words from the Cross were a glorious objective correlative to his insight in his letter to the Galatians (3:13), 'Christ redeemed us from the curse of the law by becoming the cursed one himself.'

I am not a pious person; I have failed too often not to regard myself critically. But there have been times in my life when I have felt so like Paul in the sense that after what is called his conversion and his withdrawal into the desert to brood on it, when he returns to the places on the eastern Mediterranean shores, he never goes to Jerusalem to check his understanding of Christ with those who had known him, but quarrels with Peter over the meaning of Christianity, clinging always to his new vision of it, its universality and the individual life. So in a moment of solitude I have grasped to myself an insight that I felt was uniquely mine. At such times I have felt I was going beyond Socrates, beyond Kierkegaard.

It was coming up to Christmas and the new dispensations of the *Casebook* and *Alibi* were proving surprisingly successful. I must do something in the New Year to express my gratitude.

To say that what I set myself to in 1966 was the result of a conversion would be absurd, in the profound sense of that word before Sartre trivialized it. But true conversion is the result of a long process and it is not necessarily religious. Conversion, as I saw it, was the recognition of the wholeness of one's self. Augustine was whole in this sense; Pascal before the spectacle of Port-Royal acquired wholeness. Mozart started whole; Beethoven and Wagner worked towards it. With great artists, wholeness becomes a habit of life. Not so with actors, who are always diminished creatures until their light pieces together the great work of others. We are at one remove from greatness, but at one remove we share it.

I did not feel that I was sharing my insight with anyone, because I was striding away from such art as is mine into another field, albeit the most profound in life. The field where truth grows through the weeds. The moment that sent me off on my journey was a prize-giving ceremony in a Yorkshire school where I was presenting the prizes. After the ceremony I was talking to the rector and without an appropriate seriousness I said, 'I suppose I could say that the Archimedean point of my life was Christ's words "My God, my God, why hast thou forsaken me?"' He looked at me for a moment, then, as he wandered away, he murmured, 'I wish he hadn't said that'. The words were so simple, but they opened up aeons of history, of life and experience, and as I saw it, all the layers of my sensibility were pierced. With what?

I thought that Paul's conversion and the subsequent events and arguments that are described and deployed in Paul's letters and the Acts (which does not mention the letters) sprang from an acute awareness of his individual nature against the background of Jewish and social life. The model of Paul's letters is the dialogues of Plato. His arguments are neither schematic nor doctrinal; like the Platonic dialogues they seize on a problem in the young groups as a starting point and then expand into the most profound and delicate analysis. He does not, it seems, accept Socrates's doctrine of Recollection, but goes beyond it in recognizing that identity and authenticity could only be acquired in relation to a life held in a special sense within a concept of God. So Paul could say quite simply, 'Not I, but Christ lives in me,' and such was the energy generated in his imagination that it coloured his views not only of his own mind and body, but of the whole range of experiences man lives in the world.

Kierkegaard had gone beyond Paul by rejecting the objectivity of the Church to proclaim that 'Christianity is spirit, spirit is inwardness,' an inwardness that could only be achieved by being contemporary with Christ. This concept of contemporaneousness I came to see as one of Kierkegaard's most profound insights. For given Sherrington's ideas on mind, memory and imagination as lying outside the neurophysiologist's acquisition, was there not a sense in Einstein's view of time that the mind was always now, always contemporary, and therefore not only with Christ on a cross, but with an artist at Lascaux through all human history to an actor sitting in the Savoy Theatre in London? It was not only history that had to be rethought, but chronology. The Evangelists, familiar with Paul's letters and intent on composing a life from what they could glean of it from Jews living in the small Greek communities, had seized on one element to complement Paul's inner appropriation of the man Jesus. That element was offence.

Over Christmas and into 1966 I brooded over the moments in Christ's life after the Last Supper.

Curigwen often asks me, 'DO you believe in God?' 'Put like that,' I say, 'it's a silly question. My life, my darling, begins with you, then it extends to our children, then to the grand-children, to my colleagues in the theatre, to the people of our countries, to Europe, to the World.' She seems to think that's all right.

The Last Words from the Cross go in the opposite direction. They begin with the world, then to his neighbours, then to his mother then to his thirst, then to himself, to his dereliction from God, then accepting that – his heart is gloriously open to the World, and as John saw – it was finished. It could go on the back of a postcard. Instead, I would do more. It was only when I'd given it much thought that I realized that nothing like this had ever been done before. Spirit was inwardness, the Last Words are the technique by which the spirit can be assured of inwardness. Can be assured of the offence.

Our Chaplain at the Savoy Theatre, Peter Naylor, had a parish on South Lambeth Road. He had often asked me to go down there. I don't preach. If I ever talk in church, it's a thinking aloud. One day I said to him that, if he liked, I'd conduct the Three Hours Service on Good Friday. This is the moment in the Church when there's no appropriate service and is usually given over to a meditation from twelve noon to three pm, being the time it had taken to crucify Christ. Naturally, I couldn't take the prayers. When he agreed, I devised a service interposing between the meditations short readings from Kierkegaard's *Training in Christianity*, together with Passion hymns (suitably cut – they go on and on). It was a draining process. I have done it twice since: when Bill Morris asked me to do it in Glasgow Cathedral; and at Inverness during Easter, when I was opening the Eden Court Theatre. But never again.

10 Venice

There was something absolutely ridiculous about my life at this time. An actor playing at the Savoy Theatre during the evenings of the week, rehearsing and recording stories about a Scottish doctor during the days of the week, and the rest of the time working something out about the Crucifixion. And yet no one noticed. I felt empty like John of the Cross or Simone Weil, but I was an actor. I'd done my thinking about God for a bit, and the sudden absurdity of my situation gave me thought.

What started me was the fact that I never wore make-up – in the theatre or television. This had started with the new lighting in the late fifties, when colour was more correctly harmonized in the lights, and there was no longer a need to balance the ambers and blues that shone from above with a delicate protective shading on the face. Since playing in *Inherit the Wind* I had not used make-up. And now viewers who could see me on a Sunday on television, as Dr Cameron, could on the following night come to the Savoy Theatre and see me as a Judge. The same face, the same voice? Not quite, the accent was different. But the difference was more fundamental and reflected something of my feelings about acting.

It was necessary, I think, for actors like Olivier, dedicated to the great parts in Shakespeare, to be expert in make-up, creating on their faces an objective correlative to the objective world of verse and hierarchy, but with Ibsen's world of prose and inwardness, and the growth of natural light on the stage, such concern with the face was excessive, for it is one of the paradoxes of the new prose theatre that the whole body is involved. All theatres until the twentieth century

86

followed roughly the ground design of the Greek amphitheatre, which entailed that an actor's main line of vision was upward towards the upper circles of the theatre, thus ensuring that all below could see.

But now theatres were different, as I'd experienced on the open stage of the Pembroke Theatre, Croydon. What was now important was the displacement of space, the still posture of the body, the fall of the head. In my own case, it had encouraged an idiosyncrasy of diction, so if I had to describe my acting I could say it was the comedy of inflection. Unlike the physical movement in classical plays that can change rapidly and with great variety, the aim in Ibsen's prose plays, for instance, I found to be an intent stillness. A duologue of alternating lines, listening and response. Somewhere inside me there was an absurd metaphysical sense that everyone acted, and I was involved in breaking down the barriers between life and art. So a new style of living might evolve, that could experience the levels of sensibility that I was encouraging elsewhere in my being, and observing immediately in my relations with Curigwen and the family.

At this time, I laughed a great deal at myself, at my audacity and ignorance. One Wednesday matinee, a few weeks after Easter, Henry Sherwood of the management came into my dressing-room. He told me that they wanted to close the theatre soon, because people had been tripping over the carpet in the stalls (I smiled at this, I was sure that the carpet hadn't been changed since I first appeared there in 1930). And as the play was in the middle of a successful run, it seemed an opportune time to make the alterations, the summer season not having started. 'Gosh,' I said, 'what a delightful surprise!'

'I thought you'd like it,' Henry said. 'Ten days.'

Not making up, I am out of the theatre very quickly; indeed once a performance is over, I like to get rid of it immediately.

Out of the stage door like an arrow, I darted up to my club in Garrick Street. No one was about; it was that witching hour of stillness before dinner, when men dream of the mysterious evening before them. I withdrew to a small anteroom to relax and brood on the unpredictable prospect before me. Come a quarter to seven, I wandered into the Coffee Room for a small repast. It was very dimly lit, but I could see one lonely figure sitting at the long table. As I approached it, life and art dissolved into one. It was a fellow judge, Leslie Scarman, and I felt in safe hands. I sat down beside him and explained my plight. Could he help me? Money was no object (I have seldom been so rash). He paused a moment. 'Have you ever been to Venice?' he said.

'Never.'

'Then there's only one thing you can do. You must go to Venice.'

You must stay at the Gritti Palace Hotel. And you must take a little book with you. It's called *Venice for Pleasure*, strangely it's about five walks in Venice. By a chap called J. G. Links. A furrier, I believe, who wisely has a passion for Venice.'

I noted the details and thanked him. Shortly after, he left. 'I envy you,' he said.

By a great good fortune, the ten days coincided with a short break from the *Casebook*. It was all very exciting. Marty, our older daughter, would come with us. Her sister and brother, Harriet and Johnny, were already in Italy. He was waiting to go to the London School of Economics (LSE); he had been at Westminster School and didn't want to go to any Oxbridge college where he might be in danger of meeting some of his schoolmates. Marty was studying acting with someone called Yat Malmgren, and with Christopher Fettes, who'd broken away from the Central School of Speech and Drama, Hampstead (which I still thought of as the Embassy School). They were vivid young people, full of enthusiasm. Harriet was acquiring knowledge of people and things, before entering her particular field.

I had so frequently told theologians to look to their maps that arriving in Venice, in spite of having played in *The Merchant of Venice* and *Othello*, it was something I had to tell myself. The mainstream of my thoughts about Europe had always flowed from Rome westwards, and up to the Protestant North. Just as twenty years earlier, on climbing the Acropolis steps, I'd been struck by the off-centre location of the Parthenon on the great rock, presenting a problem to me which I'd not yet solved, so now descending from the skies into a city rising from the sea I realized I was entering a space that had little meaning for me. Its reputation was familiar; but what was it based on?

The weather was glorious, and our days were passed in that easy flow that comes from unhurried purpose. I was suspended in a mental state of expectation, waiting for something to happen – very pleasurably, as it was punctuated by the arrival of the children at odd times. And always the walks. The first walk of the day from the hotel down to the Piazza, Marty striding ahead of us in her miniskirt, a fashion which had recently come in, walking through a tunnel of catcalls and whistling, unconcerned at this strange expression of approval.

We followed Links's directions fairly accurately, though he is so abundant in detail that the walks require more revisiting than we could afford. Thus we early on selected and enjoyed reflections on a small space, outside a cafe, having a coffee. After the first walk, I found he had not allowed for Venice's physical impact on me. The surprising thing about the walks is that they are, in the main, through built-up areas with canals for streets, never so extended as to tire, always turning over a bridge or into a small square. But I was struck by the dominant colours, and the elements that made up this variety, red stone and green water – the stone aggressive in its solidity, the water viscous and writhing slowly. There could not be a greater contrast to the white marble of Greek statues.

Venice was subtly invading a room of my awareness that only recently I was beginning to enter. In London, I was acutely aware of a movement in all parts of society to get rid of history in the interest of the immediate; the past got in the way of the present, memory spoiled instant pleasure. The most immediate evidence for this was our reluctance to enter Europe, and understand the confusing fields of energy that poured over it. One of these fields was appearing tentatively before me. Every time we walked into the Piazza San Marco we were faced with St Mark's with its modest domes, and every church or gallery we visited left an impression of the great energy of Renaissance painting, grounded like the place itself on subtle varieties of red before reaching the eighteenth-century delicacies of Canaletto. But usually we found not far away to balance the vividness of Titian or Tintoretto an assured tracery of Byzantine extraction.

When Athens was defeated in 404 BC by Sparta in the naval engagement not too far from Byzantium (now Istanbul), the city through the fourth century disintegrated in two directions, the first to Alexandria, recently established, to form round Euclid a centre for scientific study. The second direction was a retreat eastwards as the poets withdrew to their point of origin. It was in the land of Asia Minor below Byzantium, stretching as far as Miletus, that the Trojan War took place, where Homer and his descendants composed the first epics of European civilization, the *Iliad* and the *Odyssey*. It was this area below Byzantium that Paul and the Evangelists knew, that contained places like Ephesus, Nicaea, and Chalcedon. It was an area that Rome just touched, lured away to follow eastwards in Alexander's footsteps. It was here, in the centuries before Islam and Turkey brought firmness to the social order, that there evolved the initial Greek Orthodox churches that were later to spawn north from Byzantium into the countries bordering the Black Sea and on to Russia as far as the Ural Mountains which bound the westernmost quarter of the Russian Republic, providing de Gaulle with his vision of Europe as stretching from the Atlantic to the Urals.

Everything split. It was in the nature of things. Christianity split. Rome looked westwards and split on the subjects of science and the individual. Venice looked to the East and split on orthodoxy and a kind of barbarism that asserted itself so much that it had to be destroyed, partially at least, at the battle of Lepanto in 1571 by forces from Spain and Venice under the Pope of the day, defeating the Turks.

Rome and Paris to the west, Venice and Vienna to the east. The ebb and flow of men, ideas, beliefs; fluxions were everywhere. Starting with the mathematical calculus and physics of Newton and Leibnitz, they had been accelerated as a continually moving background to our thought and lives with such velocity that we had not yet appropriated them into the currency of our thought, thus lending to our reflection that depth which would temper our immediacy. Just as there were layers of sensibility in the mind and the memory, so there were flows in society, unpredictable and inconstant. If we were failing at all, it was in our failure to recognize that the space-time continuum of the universe required a new technique of living. At least so I thought, as I went into St Mark's to celebrate Christ's entrance into heaven as recorded by Luke in Acts of the Apostles some forty years after the event. It was now Thursday, Ascension Day.

Coming out of the cathedral we wandered along the square, looking for a place to have coffee. We found one; and as we sat down we saw, approaching us, Veronica Turleigh and James Laver. Veronica had played Gertrude in the Guthrie *Hamlet* with a gentle Irish accent and a puzzled air as though Deirdre of the Sorrows had found herself uncertainly in a Nordic stew. (I was pretty sure that Guthrie, Irish himself, had some satisfaction in the contrast between a diaphanous Irish Gertrude and a sensual Scottish Claudius.) James, her husband, an expert on costume history and a former curator in the Victoria and Albert Museum, a writer of exquisite taste, cherished his wife with the dry wit of an expert in fine jewels. She was a Roman Catholic, he thoroughly English.

We shared a table. Commenting on the morning's service, I wondered why there were so many priests crammed into the pulpit like the overflow in a Dürer print. 'Oh,' said Veronica, 'they bring them in from the provinces and just pack them in to anything they've got. So long as it's the right colour.'

Walking back to the Gritti Palace, I summed up one of the contrasts between Rome and Byzantium as that in the West we plump for painting and the mass; in the East they go for the ikon of the individual and the ritual of music.

Johnny had been in Rome with Harriet, having great difficulty in getting any reply from his application to the Vienna State Opera for Festival tickets. We summoned him to Venice. Of our three children, Johnny has the deepest layer of sensibility for music. In this he reflects something of me. As a boy in His Majesty's Theatre in Aberdeen, I had caught Barbirolli's first *Meistersinger* with the British National Opera Company – BNOC – and from roughly the same seat in the gallery Eva Turner with the Carl Rosa Opera Company had stamped her Aida on my memory. I had begun singing in the theatre, but it was a makeshift thing. I had given up any idea of singing professionally when one Saturday my father brought home a turntable gramophone with some records he had casually accepted from the salesman, having little taste in music himself. When I listened to Alexander Kipnis, a Russian bass, sing a Hugo Wolf song, I murmured to myself, 'You will never sing like that.' I knew I wouldn't, so I have never tried.

Curigwen was determined Johnny should go to Vienna, so she sent him off, suitably supplied with means. He was there for a month and attended at least thirty concerts of some kind or another. We were getting near the end of this pleasant and, for me, revealing holiday. When it began I had little idea that a new dimension of Europe would expand my interior map. This is something that is very personal, for while it may be exposed for others to look at, one can never be certain that it will make the same kind of sense for them.

As I lay back in my seat on the plane taking us home, my mind was absorbed with powerful figures of red stone being dragged out of sluggish green water. Light, time, colour – in a sense they were all the same thing. I closed my eyes.

Now that the stalls of the Savoy had been repaired so that no one was in danger of breaking their ankle, the play continued its run, for twenty months altogether. This was just before the time when it became fashionable for actors to leave successful plays after a short run in case they got bogged down. I had no idea what they were afraid of. I was intensely grateful for the work. And it was very hard.

The sixties were entering a strange field. Our society was undoubtedly open, but the trough of peace was revealing itself in strange ways. Always towards the crowd. In spite of Crick and Watson, never towards the individual. Towards indiscriminate noise. Rock music and the microphone came together for the crowd to sway in community. There was little realization that the microphone had closed space to those refinements of sound and inflection that could only be experienced in the theatre. Descartes's mind-body split was still triumphant. At the heart of this open society, the immediate needs of the body had to be satisfied; the mind lay dormant before this instant fulfilment. But the main thing that was unnoticed in all quarters of our society was the central discovery of Einstein – the nature of light.

What had prompted Einstein's investigations was the question he had early asked himself, 'What would the world look like to me if I were travelling on a beam of light?' To say that the answer he found was Relativity obscures the fundamental and terrifying detail that light travels at 186,000 miles per second, and that many scientists refused to join the Manhattan Project at Los Alamos, NM, when President Roosevelt accepted Einstein's advice that it was possible to build an atomic bomb, and that it could be done on his equation, $e = mc^2$, where c equals time, equals light, travelling at such an enormous speed. Not all scientists were bereft of imagination.

It would be absurd to say that my interest in Einstein's ideas about light had anything to do with my playing of Ibsen. But 'light' was a word, and at this time I was seeking some kind of language that would embrace the fields of science without distorting or clouding them. I was not seeking for any basic reality. Scientists were brusque enough to assure me that their view of reality was not mine.

Yet when I turned to industry, the concept of light was revealing. For instance, Newton's notion of gravity dealing with motion in the universe depended on heaviness, and this notion of heaviness underlay the first industrial revolution. The exploitation of coal and steel, ship-building and so on had provided the bulwarks on which society could be built. And with it had grown a society organizing itself by reflecting this heaviness: capitalist conglomerates, trade unions, political parties, to further their own interests.

Now new ideas of fundamental reality were taking over, revealing the new powers of electricity, atomic energy, magnetic fields. There was a real but unrecognized dichotomy between the scientific discoveries of the twentieth century and the social and political organizations inherited from the nineteenth. And nowhere was it more revealing than in the understanding of light.

When I considered the great powers of the universe, I concluded that where a society was affected by this theory of light, the movement of change within it would be very slight; a large displacement would be unnatural and catastrophic.

In the nineteenth century, Germany had led the world in science and technology. When I saw the desolation of that country in 1950, it occurred to me that in its resurgence it might well recapture a new scientific awareness. In one respect, there was amazing proof of this particular philosophy of science. When it came to reinstate trade unions in the commercial spectrum, it created few; and it confined wage negotiations to an annual occasion. Thus it limited the possible displacement in a society, which everywhere was responding to the concept of lightness, acquiring volatility, diversity and uncertainty. Einstein's minute displacement of light when subjected to a gravitational field could be reflected in an acceptable wage negotiation, without disrupting society. It was scarcely to be wondered at that the Germans, with their scientific history and social cohesion, should be pre-eminent in solving the problems presented by the new science.

Both France and Italy were similarly placed, and when the three nations came together in the European Coal and Steel Community in 1952, the Treaty of Rome, signed in 1957, could have been predicted. The fact that the European Economic Community was apparently rooted in economics obscured the grounds on which it was really founded. That was the sheer energy of Europe as a space of earth, breeding kinds of men only fulfilled when their zest of curiosity was satisfied. I realized then that I have always been a passionate European; and my present dissatisfaction with the state of Britain in its permissiveness, its greed, its search for instant fun was forcing me in a way to define to myself my own aims, and what I found in my environment to sustain them, an environment that was summed up in the one word, 'Europe'.

I could not have thought like this without the continually expanding relationship with Curigwen and the children, each now creating their own distinct path. Nor could I have contained this relationship together with the flowing currents of life that Venice brought me had I not, somewhat like Einstein, seen myself on a beam of light accelerating everything into the present moment of time, the 'now' when my thought and experience came together.

We were nearing the end of *Alibi* when I was approached by representatives of a religious press who wanted to publish my meditations on the Last Words from the Cross. This was really doubly absurd, though I accepted the request seriously enough. It was unheard of for an actor to publish such a work, the guffaw of disbelief was understandable. But the second absurdity was real enough.

I had found the period immediately after the war greatly exciting, due partly to the discovery of Kierkegaard and the recognition of his influence in Europe and Japan, on thinkers like Sartre, Heidegger and Karl Kraus, in places like Paris, Vienna and most German universities, but also to the new lease of life in biblical criticism. The insights of Darwin and Einstein (there is no room for God in a space-time continuum) had stunned theologians into an intellectual paralysis. But, following writers like Albert Schweitzer, there was an increasing interest in the historical Jesus, and the evolution of the biblical texts. At this time the BBC's Third Programme was highly enlightened. But a reaction soon set in, starting with the Pope's encyclical of 1950, *Humani Generis*, condemning existentialism, revealing a risible ignorance about the nature of existentialist thought. A. J. Ayer, with a similarly closed mind, found Sartre's *Being and Nothingness* a misunderstanding of the verb 'to be'. Thus, while Kierkegaard was rejected by the Anglican Establishment as the 'gloomy Dane', in a strange way biblical criticism flourished, even to the extent of questioning the chronology of the books of the New Testament – at least until the mid-sixties, when the differences between the conservative and radical elements in the Church emerged in public statements about their views. Having experienced the chill of biblical criticism, the clergy preferred the warmth of their surplices; and by the end of the decade it might never have happened. Its place was taken by a fundamentalism, that was instant, enthusiastic, young, and always with a crowd.

What had prompted me to brood on the Last Words were Kierkegaard's views on the inwardness of spirit, the paradox that always lay at the heart of self-knowledge, and my feeling that the Last Words could only be understood now, in the present moment of time, as a pattern of inwardness.

Kierkegaard had found the pattern in the life of the New Testament as a paradox. I had given particularity to the paradox by giving the Last Words a pattern. Someone must have noticed it. Apart from a few articles in the *Church Quarterly* on the Austrian linguistic philosopher Ludwig Wittgenstein, another of my interests at this time, I had had nothing published. It was interesting, and absurd. *Alibi* ended and we took the play out on a short tour. It was now 1967.

While leaving others to the editing of the meditation, my time on tour was taken up with the confusion that existed around me; beginning with the confusion in the theatre. There have been only three great periods in history in which the flow of the theatre participated, giving its own particular colour. In Athens in the fifth century, around 460 BC, the Greek discovery of language was married to a special social awareness and a speculative energy to give birth to a specific element in life, tragedy. Aeschylus and his colleagues Sophocles and Euripides created, and were masters of, a new kind of art. Two thousand years later, a very short time in civilization, on the banks of the Thames, through a sort of subterranean subconscious, a similar wonder was created by Shakespeare. After three hundred years in Europe, Ibsen transformed this wonder of transcendent verse into universal prose. What was common to the three great periods was that they occurred in times of unblurred light, a sort of stillness before creation. As sure as Plato follows Euripides, Newton succeeds Shakespeare. Shortly before Ibsen's death, Einstein presented the world with his Special Theory of Relativity, which in 1905 no one understood; two years later, in Aberdeen on Christmas Day in 1907, I was born, obscure and unnoticed. The flux of it all. Absurdity was the universal ground.

I now deemed that we were in a period of confusion. It began, this time of confusion as far as the British were concerned, with what is euphemistically called the granting of independence to India and Pakistan in 1947. Within twenty years a great empire had been dissolved. The melting pot of races had been given a completely new dimension. The first evidence of the melting pot in the modern world was the stream of immigrants from Europe into the United States in the nineteenth and early twentieth centuries, but most of these immigrants had shared the culture of Europe and were of the same colour. Now the United Kingdom was open to a diversity of people of different colours and religion, as the dissolution spread to Asia, Africa and the Caribbean states.

In the postwar era there were two wars that stopped short of being global, in Korea (1950–53) and Vietnam (1959–75). Once cleared, the Far East became the large source of manpower for the new light industries that were to challenge Europe and America. Britain, having exhausted her foreign reserves to fight the war, and foolishly desirous of maintaining an international posture, had declined the resources that the United States through the Marshall Plan was pouring into Europe.

The Canadian media theorist Marshall McLuhan could describe the world as an electronic global village, mainly because the new fields of energy carried communications round the globe at incredible speeds. In the crushed confusion in this village, there was no place for that stillness in which the theatre burgeons. The emphasis was now on a repetition to register an identity. Parallel with this dense undergrowth, there was a spate of new theatres to satisfy civic pride, and in education, after the Robbins Report of 1964, universities sprouted everywhere to initiate the deprived into the glories of civilization. Everywhere there was a failure to analyse, and synthesize.

I was in an extremely fortunate position, having, as it were, two ears to the ground. After the tour of the play, I decided to concentrate on the television. The *Casebook*, in so far as it dealt with medicine at a particular time, constantly reminded me of change. In the fifties, my imagination had been fired by Ventris and my understanding of the revolution needed to incorporate his insights into how we viewed the origins of European civilization. In the sixties, Crick and Watson's construction of the double helix struck me more immediately. DNA was not merely the substance of life. It signalled the uniqueness of the individual. We are all unique and different, and there did not seem to be any occupant of the village to realize that Power had corrupted absolutely.

If my analysis was absurdly simplistic, the synthesis I sought in science was outrageous. At least it was to the scientist, who totally rejected the use of words to describe his activity. It was generally agreed at this time amongst all the powers that if nuclear weapons prohibited global war, explosions of a local nature were understandable as the result of either a nostalgia for the past or a longing for the future. But one event at this time struck an unsympathetic chord: the revolt of the students, expressed most effectively as one would expect in the events of May 1968 in Paris, France. And it was the Roman Catholic students in France who gave a particularity to the frustration that underlay the confusion. Marching up the Champs-Elysées, they followed a banner which carried the words, 'We must reinvent the Church'. It was not merely the Church that had to start again; the radical discoveries by science in every field demanded new structures to accommodate them. Indeed it was this recognition that lay at the heart of the confusion. It was a protest against repetition. It was absurd of Jean-Louis Barrault to appear on the stage of Odéon Theatre, and shout that he was on their side. Though he was a charming man, a moment's reflection would have told him that he represented just the sort of repetition against which they were protesting. What was interesting about the students' protest was first that it did not really spread to the rest of society, and the students never conceived a programme out of the repetition that they were protesting against. The instant, by definition, has no depth.

For the two organizations in Europe that relied totally on repetition were also the most powerful, the established Church, Catholic and Protestant, on one hand, and on the other, the Communist Party of Russia. Both were sustained by the belief that the truth had been revealed once and for all time. The Christian Church constantly rested its authority on its founder, and the doctrines needed to sustain the structure of the Church. The Communist Party rested its practice on the insights of Marx as seen by Engels and Lenin. Both Church and Party found it extremely difficult to resist making claims of totality and universality.

Unless on a matter of generality, such as evolution, those who speak for such organizations must exercise great care if they are to avoid embarrassment. In 1543, Copernicus published his *De revolutionibus orbium coelestium* (*On The Revolutions of the Heavenly Spheres*). It was adventurous for Martin Luther to declare that Copernicus was a fool, and then go on, 'Did not Holy Writ declare that it was the sun, not the earth, which Joshua commanded to stand still?' Brecht, in his play, *The Life of Galileo*, put a vivid phrase into Galileo's mouth, 'He to whom the eternal word speaketh, is relieved of much questioning'. I remembered between the wars the sympathy I felt for those Russians who had to accept Stalin's view of comprehensiveness when he sponsored Lysenko's attempt to prove that crops grew according to his Lamarckian interpretation of Marxist–Leninist principles, and not the genetic laws of Mendel. In much the same way, in the nineteenth century Cardinal Newman, who I'm sure was a gentle man, could say that the Roman Catholic Church did not need the Bible. It had the doctrines.

But at least there was de Gaulle. The students' revolt signalled his withdrawal from politics. What it could not do was to erase the stamp he had imposed on France, and to make his country the knot around which the other European nations hovered. His decision that France should have its own nuclear force and produce its own energy was a model decision for any politician determined to ensure his country's independence. I have not heard of any French politician of any party who would remove these pillars of a French identity. The effect of de Gaulle's decision was scarcely noticed among politicians, and certainly not in Britain which had not begun to think of the technique required to live with the new realities.

New techniques do not emerge like Athene, fully armed. Civilization is too wary. In the flow of new ideas anywhere, whether it is from Rome westward, or the arc of Byzantine orthodoxy, new ideas have their swaddling clothes which have to be carefully unwrapped. For it is one thing to see the new, it is quite another to understand what it's about. What was original about de Gaulle's decision (and I don't think he knew what he was doing) was demonstrating how the technique of lightness could be applied to society, and how this radically affected politics and religion. As seen from England, it has always been a mystery how France and Italy could maintain a tolerable equilibrium with such enormous Communist Parties within their frontiers. A similar situation in Britain would have resulted in revolution.

11 The Greek Experience

The theatre, like society, was being atomized. There was always the Royal Court, trying to repeat the tradition of innovation inherited from Granville-Barker. But even the various subsidized theatres were extending their programmes into commercial areas, blurring the distinctiveness of the noncommercial theatre image, which had always depended on Shakespeare. And an actor's career lapped over from the theatre into radio, films and television, with a consequent cannabalizing of technique; a benign naturalism spread over all the media despite the fundamental differences.

Against this splitting in society there was always our family, Curigwen's warmth presided over and encouraged these slight divergences in nature which were emerging as they grew older. The girls were moving into different areas of the theatre; Johnny, now at LSE, spent most of his time in the library while other students were demonstrating.

It may have been that I was early impressed by Karl Popper's *The Open Society and its Enemies*, but I have always loathed cliques, a malign growth that thrives in the theatre; with some reason, perhaps, as the early actor-managers of the sixteenth century drew their companies round about them in hierarchical descent. But these times were past; the grounds of democracy were freedom and openness. So that when we started rehearsing the *Casebook* I suggested to Barbara Mullen and Bill Simpson that we should sit in different parts of the rehearsal room so that the atmosphere of the rehearsals would always be open. It was absurd but I felt that in this openness there lay the space and light for difference to be seen and growth to emerge; something which was not possible with the crowd.

It was at this time that I became acutely aware of the stature of the figure I was creating on television. Normally, appearances on television are the herald for that familiarity which reduces difference to a common ground of understanding. People share the performance; the church has much to bear for introducing the concept of the vicarious.

I was approached by the Chairman of the London Committee of the British Medical Association (his name was Cameron!) to be the guest of honour at the annual dinner of the BMA. It was normal for the guest to make a speech. When Dr Cameron asked me what I was going to talk about, after a pause I blithely said, 'Oh, Instant Diagnosis!' If it interested him, it also confused him, because he invited me to his club in Pall Mall, overtly to explain the procedure, covertly to explore what I meant by Instant Diagnosis. I explained.

This was the first opportunity I'd had to explore what playing Dr Cameron meant to me, and to suggest the, to them, somewhat tenuous connection between art and medicine. I was still preoccupied with my early justification for my profession, that art was the solution to problems that could not be solved in any other way, and I was very conscious of the prejudice against actors invading such fields. What kind of problems had I in mind?

In the event, I told them how I had come to play Cameron; his time, his country, and his situation as a country doctor of thirty years in practice, and, this was most important, knowing nothing of penicillin.

My point was that what I called Instant Diagnosis arose from my knowledge, as Cameron, of the history of the families I was treating. Nature is economical in disease as in everything, and the moment a patient from my practice stepped into my surgery a machine in my mind registered the range of sickness that was possible. I contrasted this with the patients the contemporary doctor treats, unfamiliar with the family history in our volatile society. Symptoms are treated out of a liberal pharmacopoeia that was not available to Cameron in Scotland. Failing a suitable prognosis, the patient of today can always be referred to a specialist for treatment. It is the new kind of instant medicine. It is not reprehensible but reflects the kind of change that was overtaking all society.

To realize the consequences of moving out of the flat world into a curvilinear universe was very difficult. That bodies could act on each other at a distance without any apparent cause. That matter subject to heat could generate new organisms. That we were now in a universe without purpose, inheriting with nature an urge to live.

If I saw penicillin as the threshold to our new world, it was only because during the war army surgeons would rejoice that we had now

99

found the answer to the festering of wounds. As I remember it, the first intimation that nature was beginning a new dialogue was a widespread epidemic of polio. Within twenty years a completely new range of sickness in the nerves, the muscles, the blood had exploded with evolutionary pace. The medical disciplines of immunology, virology, and epidemiology assumed new significance by increasing the tendency towards specialization. And every increase in specialization limited the specialist's ability to synthesize. The specializations of science, in biology and physics, were depriving the scientist of his ability to analyse and synthesize for the common good. The failure was most evident after the discovery of DNA. Within years, genetic engineering and molecular biology were evolving, apparently unaware of the fields of morality and ethics they were ploughing up.

Was there in art some sort of answer to these problems that the scientist was throwing up? If I had not been playing, in the *Casebook*, a doctor at a particular time and place, I doubt if these problems would have appeared so vivid to me. Nor would they have appeared so clearly to me if I had not been steeped in the Greek experience. For the Greeks were the first people to recognize the gap between the artist and the scientist; and providing a way by which the two could be reconciled enormously enriched the range of experience. The moral we now see as the individual at the most sensitive point of his self-awareness, the ethical as the individual expressing that sensitivity with others. Both aspects dominate and permeate Greek tragedy. The evolution of that tragedy is just as distinct as the evolution of the spheres. Knowledge of both is derived by people for people. I was slowly being driven to see the great need for art, that while it entertained it somehow lay beyond mere entertainment. An art that involved life.

Some time later Harley Williams, the first director of the newly amalgamated Chest, Heart and Stroke Association (CHSA) of the BMA, asked me to speak at the setting-up of a new branch in Glasgow. After that he invited me to join the Council.

In the last years of the sixties, the *Casebook* was recorded in Glasgow, where new studios had just been built. It meant an addition to my confusion. For apart from the instantaneous noise without which society apparently could not exist, there was now added a national dimension which had been lying dormant for some time. But being away from home was not as disturbing as it might have been. The family were on the point of completing their formal education. We had introduced them to Europe and they were in due course to explore North America by courtesy of the Greyhound Bus.

I come from the east coast of Scotland and over the years my flow of awareness was towards Scandinavia. I now called myself a Protestant Anglican, and my radical views mostly derived from Norway and Scandinavia, filtered through the many colours of Europe. I had in the fifties paid two fleeting visits to Scotland, to Glasgow to record two of Bridie's plays, *Dr Angelus* and *Meeting at Night* at the old studios in Parkhead, near the Celtic football ground. But now there was a new generation and a new restlessness, as we were approaching the painful volatility of the seventies.

There is a greater toughness in Scottish acting than I could find in my English colleagues, and this gave a backbone to the playing of characters in the painful state of Scotland in the twenties and thirties. I also met many Scottish actors who felt the need of a national dimension in the theatre. There were in many Scottish towns substantial theatres, inherited from the past, that could accommodate normal touring plays, and there was, in the present, the gloriously idiosyncratic Citizens' Theatre, initiated by Bridie, which, while creating a national focus, spread over the borders internationally.

The *Casebook* drew to its close on television in 1969, continuing on radio. Before doing anything else we decided to return to Greece. It was part of the world where I had courted Curigwen in 1939. My awareness of Greece had expanded enormously, and there were places like Troy, Mycenae, and Knossos that we had not visited. My intelligence needed this stimulus. In 1969, we embarked on a Swan's tour in the company of the archaeologist Mortimer Wheeler and the historian Owen Chadwick, truly excellent guides.

Although we'd visited Delphi and Athens with the Old Vic company in the spring of 1939, my most vivid memory of that visit, apart from classical actress Katina Paxinou's right tit peeping through her woven dress, was my first view of the Parthenon when at the top of the Acropolis steps I'd turned to Curigwen and said, 'Why is it there?' It was a question that had kept recurring in my mind during the war, and I had a vague idea I might find an answer. The problem was quite simple. The Parthenon does not stand on the centre of the great rock, in spite of being the temple of Athene. It stands down to the right-hand corner. Why?

Following Ventris, it had been impossible to confine myself to biblical studies; so that all the time in *Alibi* my reading was divided between

101

the Greeks, biblical studies and others. Woven into this pattern were considerations of acting, words, the nature of knowledge, and always, derived from Sherrington, what he approaches all the time in his *Man on his Nature* but does not touch, the nature of mind, memory and imagination.

We began with a surprise. At Istanbul I had no idea that there was so much power in water until I saw the Bosphorus, that flows between two seas and, in a way, between two continents. I thought of that early ship, the Greek trireme, the three-layered ship; it must have been strong and light to navigate such waters.

Layers, layers ... the nine layers of Troy, the widening circles, as each dynasty built on past ruins, in such an uninviting surrounding. And the river Scamander! A trickle of syllables that meandered to the sea, yet culled from Rupert Brooke a marvellous place in the last line of his double sonnet, *Menelaus and Helen*: 'And Paris slept on by Scamander side'. Why was this derelict place so significant in the old world? I could only think of one reason. It guarded the entrance to the Bosphorus. Whoever controlled Troy commanded access to the fruitful fields of wheat as we see them now in Romania and the Ukraine. Twice it had been significant. Once, when the Greek princess Helen had been abducted by the Trojan prince Paris; that was the metaphor the poets found for a political adventure. The second when Athenian ships followed Spartan ships towards this place, and were destroyed in 404 BC, the grim year that tolled the bell for the democracy of Athens. Yet it was round here that much of the art migrated when the city was defeated. Round here were places with names like Nicaea, Ephesus, Chalcedon that were to loom up as the early Christian Fathers sought to bring some Greek light to the intractable Latin in search of a doctrine.

To Aspendos, where Mortimer Wheeler persuaded me to do something in the theatre. After some hesitation and placing Curigwen halfway up in the auditorium, I pitched a reading of that Shakespeare sonnet that begins, 'Shall I compare thee to a summer's day?' The acoustics were apparently superb; Wheeler, in the front row, and Curigwen heard me perfectly.

Knossos, originally, Kinossos, followed. The placid forecourt, with the bronze head of Arthur Evans on a pedestal, scarcely prepares one for the amazing sophistication of the palace, and its focus as the main centre of the currents that were to whirl round Europe between the cave drawings of Lascaux and Athenian tragedy. The palace was destroyed sometime between 1400 and 1300 BC. The fire that followed baked much of the evidence on which the pre-eminence of Knossos exists. The revelation of the contents of the palace was only realized at the end of the nineteenth century, and they are still under investigation.

The archaeologist divides the periods of time into civilizations, thus Minoan, followed by Mycenaean and so on into the Dark Ages. I looked at things very differently. While clearly, Crete and Mycanae had stamped their names on the succeeding civilizations, somewhere in the centuries there enters a people from no specific area whom we now call Greek, leaping forward like that early artist at Lascaux with certain perceptions about life and what they could bring to it. The perceptions were bound up with the nature of matter, particularly stone and what could be wrought with it, and sound and its relevance for language, especially diction. From Crete in the south to Troy in the north, spanning the islands of the Aegean, the Greek element in the civilizations brought a sensitivity about life that lay outside the wayward movements of power.

The first murmurs of Hellenic civilization that archaeology reveals to us were the tablets of Knossos, deciphered in my own lifetime, and the heroic epics of Homer shaping themselves round Troy. The shaping of stone came later. And the startling notion that all language begins with verse, reflecting the rhythmic beat of the foot as the body responds to the beat in the sound. All sound given length acquires beat. In this the vowel is dominant arising from an open throat. The vowels would rampage all over the place, were they not given measure and structure by the staccato beat of the consonant and syllable, a sound that can only be made by a closed throat.

The cave drawings at Lascaux and Altamira (at Lascaux only discovered in 1940 by children playing) reveal the eye cooperating with the imagination and the memory to portray the external world. It took centuries for the memory and the imagination to combine the two elements of sound, its making and its hearing. And then it could only relate to the external world through signs such as the symbols on the tablets at Knossos, preserved for us by chance, and only deciphered some fifteen years before. Symbols representing the humblest physical things, that make up the inventory of a larder or store.

It was absurd that I, an actor, should brood about these things. Yet it was precisely because I was an actor that I could brood about them in this way. In an extraordinary way, my mind had become so saturated with what people called the Greek experience that I could project my imagination back, and see their problems as they saw them, and how they came to their solution.

Approaching Mycenae from the south, I was conscious of a repetition of things. The flat land, the high sky, the distant hills reminded me of the plain of Beauce, south-west of Paris, that lies before the rise of

Chartres Cathedral. Just before we reach the place itself a road turns off to the left towards Corinth. Beyond Corinth lies Lepanto (now Návpaktos). With that memory, Venice asserted itself in contrast, the red cavern of the city, the viscous green canals, that enveloped one in density. Here everything was light and openness.

And then the surprise of the lion gate, the rough path up to the Acropolis, great in reputation but domestic in proportion. Were the ruts in the path first made when Agamemnon brought Cassandra here in his chariot after the end of the Trojan conflict? The ruts are very deep, the Acropolis not imposing. We climbed slowly to the top. After Athens, Mycenae is small and compact. While both existed at the time of the Trojan War, it took the Greeks hundreds of years to learn what to do with the great mass of rock that is the Acropolis of Athens. Everything that comes into being has a history. Looking round I had little doubt that some of the great innovations that make Athens the primary citadel of Europe began here.

There was, first, the view towards the hills. An actor could not but be deeply moved. I was standing near the spot where Clytemnestra stands at the beginning of the *Agamemnon* of Aeschylus, waiting, looking towards the distant hills, the Watchman on the proscenium arch behind her. Suddenly comes his barbaric cry as the beacons begin to shine in the night. I looked down to the ground where I was standing. I became very still. I gaped.

Mycenae shared with Athens the goddess Athene. An archaeologist had drawn on the ground the lines of her temple. Next to it he had drawn the lines of the royal palace (that is, the megaron, or hall), the round base of the building where the king held his receptions. Their proximity created an image in my imagination that forced my memory back to our first visit to the Acropolis. That first visit when I looked over the great rock towards the Parthenon, and asked Curigwen, 'Why is it there?'

Was it like that in Athens because it had been first like that in Mycenae? I felt like Schliemann when he looked down on the mask of Agamemnon. But there was no King of Prussia to whom I could send my problem. I thought it out.

By the second half of the sixth century, Pisistratus had performed his great work of organizing the *Iliad* and the *Odyssey* and, like many others later, thought a drama festival would benefit everyone. The site would be the present theatre of Dionysus, now in ruins. There was no royal palace for Pisistratus on the great rock. The nearest Athens got to providing a palace was the megaron, the floor of the theatre, the orchestra, the dancing place where the actors and chorus performed.

104

There had been a Parthenon, or temple to Athene; but it was never allowed to last long, owing to the habit of the Persians in their wars with the Greeks of destroying the monuments of the Acropolis. Eventually, when Athens had finally defeated the Persians, Pericles decided to rebuild the Parthenon to the glory of its goddess, using the greatest artists of the day. But with one great difference. Instead of building on the old site, he decided to move it over the sacred way to a position much closer to the theatre of Dionysus. The Greek theatre had by this time, the 430's BC, reached a position of enormous prestige. The clearing up of texts by Pisistratus had presented the dramatists with such an abundance of material that it has lasted to this day.

Why did Pericles want to see the Parthenon and the theatre of Dionysus, so clearly reproducing the situation at Mycenae, in such close proximity? The home of the virgin goddess and the site of offensive tragedy! Did he see the buildings as physical symbols of the innocence and offence that are the beginning and end of existence? Was he measuring in some way the limits of civilization that had been the burden of Greek thought since Troy, a thought that had been transformed by the Jews into a different image, a different movement from offence to innocence? From innocence to offence, from offence to innocence? As an actor I had to live with both movements.

The family was breaking up – in the best possible way, they were becoming independent. The girls left home; only Johnny remained. He had graduated from LSE, taking a BSc in economics. Coming to me one day, he said he didn't want to be an academic, couldn't be a tycoon; he wanted to go into the theatre. This was astonishing because he didn't want to be an actor. He hated acting, but the technique of the theatre, its management, interested him. He has not acted, but his experience in the theatre and its branches has been enormous.

I had become chairman of the Scottish Actors Company. A group of us, Fulton Mackay, Roddy Macmillan, Una McLean, Alex McCrindle, Cochrane Duncan, faced with the great diversity around us, thought a space should be found for a Scottish, distinctive voice. It was really born out of a particular enthusiasm provided by Bridie and the Citizens' Theatre. We were aware of the fragments of society broken up by the appeal of the new range of entertainment, radio, film, television, theatre. And acutely conscious of language, as between English, Scots, Lallans. And ultimately the roots of identity. English and French identity in the modern world had been given strong roots in the sixteenth and seventeenth centuries by drama, by Shakespeare in

England, and Corneille and Racine in France. (This was really a memory of Greece; the art of Aeschylus and his colleagues gave Athens a firm bridgehead into experience.) This had been provided by a common source that each country had discovered for itself, a diction that fitted drama. Because it fitted drama, this language became the ground of communication. I had just returned from Greece, and was acutely aware of the failure of Latin to replace Greek. This was most evident in the failure to produce any dramatist of substance to compare with the Athenian playwrights. After the comedy of Aristophanes, Plautus and Terence were feeble; and Seneca, although following tragic Greek models, was never produced in his lifetime.

The closeness of England had through the centuries created an ambivalent attitude to the language which had done much to stamp a moderating phlegm on the people, in contrast to the irrational, violent Scots. While we had many dialects we had no overriding language. When our thinkers practised philosophy, they wrote in English. Yet, when our actors used English they revealed an idiosyncrasy (as in Duncan Macrae and Alastair Sim), and toughness that was not natural to the English character. It was something of this that we wanted to present.

The idea of the Company was tolerably well received, so that it presented *The Wild Duck* at the Edinburgh Festival of 1970, directed by Fulton Mackay. Bridie always held that Henrik Ibsen was a Scottish dramatist – whose real name was Henry Gibson. The following year, we joined with Henry Sherwood to present *The Douglas Cause* by William Douglas Home; Fulton and I appeared in this, a domestic, legal controversy out of the past of the Home family. It eventually came to the Duke of York's Theatre, but without great success.

Our next project was to be a play by C. P. (Cecil) Taylor in which I was to appear, the idea being that it would initially tour the large Scottish theatres. The play was appropriate, but it soon became clear that the funding from the Scottish Arts Council would not be adequate to cover production costs and any loss that might occur. They would not help in production costs – the most they could do was to guarantee up to £5000 against any loss we might incur. At first, I was prepared to help; but in spite of the careful costing of Alex McCrindle, it became clear that if the play was not an overwhelming success, a great deal of money might be lost. I simply did not have these resources. And, after much heartsearching, I told my colleagues that I could not do the play. It was a deep disappointment to them, a deeper one for Cecil Taylor; and for me it brought a profound sense of failure, which occupies a permanent place in my sensibility. My colleagues were successful actors, and were engaged in other enterprises. Cecil Taylor was a born drama-tist, and it was with some delight that later I saw that the Royal Shakespeare Company (RSC) had taken him under their wing.

The sixties had been the decade of the instant without reflection. My experience indicated that something new was happening in the seventies. Our society was becoming truly volatile, extremely vulnerable to money. It was the decade of cashflow. It was absurd that I, an actor, should learn this so painfully.

12 Ibsen and Munich

Richard Eyre had become director of the Lyceum Theatre in Edinburgh and asked me to do Solness again in *The Master Builder*. I supposed that if one endured, nature could always be guaranteed to come up with something new, even repetition.

I had been so preoccupied with discoveries about the world and myself that I hardly noticed that my little book on the Last Words from the Cross had been published under the title *The Infinite Guarantee*. I now found some irony in the use of that word 'guarantee'. It did, however, produce some balm. Although it went completely unnoticed (it was really surprising that neither the *Scotsman* nor the *Glasgow Herald* deigned to review it), William Neil, Reader in Biblical Studies at Nottingham University, found it 'a very remarkable book'. He added: 'I can only describe it as a little masterpiece.' The book was a consideration of the last words from a Greek view. I was very grateful to Dr Neil, and assured that someone in the theological establishment was familiar with the source of Christianity. I don't think the publishers were too excited. We were at the beginning of that enthusiastic crowd of Christians that I found repulsive.

I had better luck with the play. Richard had cast Susan Macready as Hilda and Joyce Heron as Mrs Solness. I have been extremely fortunate in the women who have played opposite me in Ibsen. Once again, it was a delight to play Ibsen lightly, and the exercise in avoiding rhetoric was exhilarating. After a short run, Curigwen and I decided to join her brother Ivor, who was now retired and living in Majorca, in a flat at Valldemosa, which he rented from a German resident in Munich. Graves was still living at Deyá, but though tempted to visit him, I never did. During the war I'd done my officer training with his son David, who was later killed. I was once asked by a commanding officer why I'd gone into the Royal Welch Fusiliers instead of the Gordon Highlanders. I told him that I was married to a Welsh wife, and that the Fusiliers was perhaps the most literary regiment in the British Army, having after the First World War produced two authors, Robert Graves (*Goodbye to All That*) and Siegfried Sassoon (*Memoirs of an Infantry Officer*), whose work I greatly admired. He sniffed and turned away; he didn't like it. Graves and Sassoon had become pacifists. I don't really mind what people think. I didn't much mind when Ivor made his oblique criticism of my Last Words book. Christianity was not a pattern, he said.

Later that year (1972) we were to join him in Munich. His German landlady also had a flat in Schwabing and gave it to him for the period of the Olympic Games. A holiday! We were a walk's distance from the centre of Munich. Not too early, after struggling with the radio to get the English news, and a breakfast of coffee, rolls and butter, we would wander down to the art galleries of Munich. There were, of course, the Impressionists – they get everywhere. But here, there were even more Kandinskys, Kokoschkas, and *Der blaue Reiter* Expressionist painters. No smudges or mists here, but every detail expressed with energy and passion. This was the other side of art, that looked away from Paris towards Vienna. I had almost forgotten this.

After the war, Curigwen and I used to visit Paris every two years, just to reassure ourselves how good the French theatre was. We always stayed at the Hotel de Nice in the Rue des Beaux Arts on the Left Bank, just opposite the hotel where Oscar Wilde once lived. At the end of our street was the Rue de Seine; and at the top of it was Les Deux Magots, a café where Sartre was supposed to go. But we never saw him.

Our first morning in Paris was always spent crossing the Seine to the Louvre; in the afternoon down the Tuileries gardens to the Orangerie to see the Impressionists. Then in the evenings Barrault at the Marigny, Jouvet in *Tartuffe* at the Étoile, Edith Piaf at Olympia. And always, once, duck at the Tour d'Argent. We no longer know how to cook duck.

Round these experiences there grew in my mind the notion of Paris at the turn of the century, a vortex of creation in art and science, in music and sculpture. So strong was this notion that it obliterated the rest of Europe. And now, Vienna.

Over the three weeks of our stay in Munich, we had booked to go to four of the Olympic events. One day, 5 September, after visiting a gallery, and enjoying a modest lunch in the open air, we found a taxi to take us through Schwabing to the Olympic Stadium for the athletics. We had just passed Schwabing when we are stopped, all traffic was stopped. There was shouting. Why the stoppage? Then there seemed to be a moment's quiet. Out of the silence we heard that the Games had been cancelled for the day. Just before midday, the greater part of the Israeli team had been murdered by members of the PLO. Persons, athletes, Jews had been murdered. Individuals. Dazed, we participated in the mourning – and the Games went on. The urge to live was incessant in its onward flow. W. B. Yeats says, in *The Second Coming*, 'Things fall apart; the centre cannot hold ...' Here I was at Munich, almost the centre between Paris and Vienna, observing that move which really began in the seventies, here in Munich, and will go on and on as long as people remember Hiroshima, the note of terror that can be exercised by the few on the individual. This was the sort of war that could be sanctioned by great powers held at bay by their fearful imaginations.

And always this terror was justified by its righteousness, the perpetrators always justified their actions as being in a just cause! It was individuals who were suffering. This in spite of Crick and Watson's double helix that proclaimed the uniqueness of each individual. I did not believe that science would prove the salvation of mankind, as Eddington thought when Rutherford split the atom. With Shakespeare, I thought that all the men and women were merely players; and when they realized that, they would see that life was an art, and desire to practice it, rejoicing in their new creations. As I did. This was really mad. I had no way of proving it. Except by the absurd, that nobody would believe.

Returning home, my memory had expanded to carry the tragedy of the Munich Olympics, and was to go on expanding through the decade as other groups in other places, and nearer home in Northern Ireland, were to practise what I now saw as the ultimate sin in society – the destruction of the individual. Even science must concur in that.

There was still work for the BBC. From being a doctor between the wars, I had now graduated to being a solicitor in some unspecified border town in Scotland with my two colleagues from the *Casebook*. It was a transition easily accomplished, since the stories and writing were in the hands of Donald Bull, a man of great accomplishment and sensitivity.

It was getting towards the end of 1972 when I was approached by Jenny Carter of Johnston and Bacon, a subsidiary in Scotland of the publishing house of Cassell and Collier Macmillan. She wanted me to write something about Scotland – *Andrew Cruickshank's Scottish Bedside*

Book? I think Jenny thought I would produce a book of stories that would occupy a place in hotel bedrooms alongside the Gideon Bible. However, I didn't see it quite like that. For years I had believed with Kierkegaard that communication in all spheres except science should be indirect, leaving the individual to appropriate the truth of the matter for himself as he recognized it. This required some art in communication. After a little brooding I agreed to undertake a *Scottish Bedside Book*. But it would be, I thought, a little unusual, perhaps; it would be about my people.

In the sixties, the writing of history in Britain in any new sense had all but disappeared under the powerful examples of political historians Lewis Namier and the Marxist Christopher Hill, who confined themselves to the histories of men in institutions, thus conveying how politics had come about. From France there were new ideas emerging. History in depth, as historians examined the layers of areas through which a community expressed its living, religion, economics, territory and so on. The masterpiece in this connection had just been translated into English, Fernand Braudel's *The Mediterranean and the Mediterranean World in the Age of Philip II* (1973), centring on Spain in the sixteenth century. Its detail was enormous, and could not possibly serve me as a model. I was not an academic nor had I the time to do the research. Thomas Smout was doing this kind of social history in Scotland. I would have to contrive my own method. I was becoming aware of an acute difference in Scottish and English education. I had been asked to join the London Society for the Study of Religion, a small group of all religions that met in the Athenaeum three times a year to discuss some specialist paper.

Both here and at the Council meetings of the CHSA, I realized how specialized English education had become, in that none of the experts involved seemed to be aware or capable of the synthesis that was increasingly needed to blend their different strands together. I had noticed this to be a development of evolution itself. Evolution is a universal process in life, yet its initial revelation is always minimal, scarcely ever more than two components. But, given these, the urge to live, as Sherrington saw, was rapid and diverse. Light could be seen as lines, or waves and particles; genes, as compounded of protein and nucleic acid. Once movement and heat was introduced, evolution was rapid into lines which were complicated and required intense study, with a consequent loss of the awareness of the whole. This seemed to me to be the state of English thinking at the time. I would divide this book into two parts. The first, 'The Line', how Scotland had grown through the centuries; secondly, 'The Mosaic', the things that Scotsmen

111

had achieved in the world that surrounded us. And always through people. And nothing too long or heavy. It took years to assemble the material, and pleasurable times at the London Library.

1973 was only a few months old when John Gale asked me to take over from Ralph Richardson at the Savoy Theatre in William Douglas Home's play *Lloyd George Knew My Father*. The play was following the new fashion of recasting at modest intervals. Richardson and Celia Johnson were doing something else. This was the first time I'd met John Gale since George Fearon had persuaded him to join Peter Bridge to go into management for the first time and present *Inherit The Wind* at the St Martin's Theatre. My wife in the play was to be Avice Landon, an actress with a delicious edge in comedy and a sense of self-mockery. Douglas-Home writes so well that playing in this sort of comedy can become a self-indulgence, unless disciplined. Avice had a similar professional sense, and playing with her was like juggling with mock rapiers.

This time at the Savoy my preoccupations were with the *Bedside Book* which was slowly taking shape. Miss Evans had become George Eliot, and Kierkegaard's first works were produced under pseudonyms. No one would take a bedside book seriously, therefore I could be serious; for instance, in the case of the Royalist soldier-poet Lord Montrose and the physicist Clerk Maxwell. Besides, I thought that the instant preoccupations of the sixties with its accompanying noise had banished history, and the seventies, apart from drawing attention to our nakedness and uncertainty, were being extremely revealing about the vulnerabilities of science.

James D. Watson had been persuaded by the former director of the Cavendish Laboratory, Sir Lawrence Bragg, to tell the story of the double helix, revealing the petty jealousies, envy, ambition and pain that surrounded the story. Einstein's Special Theory of 1905 had been greeted as incredible. And in this country we knew of Rutherford's dismissal of nuclear fission. Science was on the way to deflating the trust that everyone put in it. And behind it was the growing feeling everywhere that Hiroshima would never be repeated.

In the theatre, costs are adjusted weekly. When balanced, box-office receipts must exceed what is known as the get-out – the cost plus minimum profit which must be made in the week. Our takings towards the end of the year dipped for two weeks below the get-out figure, and we had to leave the Savoy.

We moved to the St Martin's Theatre! My arc of theatre after the war had been provided in the West End of London, shuttling here and there. But there was a recurrence of shuttling between the Savoy and the St Martin's that was becoming ridiculous. John Gale had transferred *Inherit the Wind* to the St Martin's, and years later he was transferring a play I was in to the St Martin's. And both theatres were caught up in the private investigations that kept my mind busy. At the end of *Inherit the Wind* I stood on the stage as Clarence Darrow balancing two books in my hands – the Bible and Darwin's *The Origin of Species*. At the Savoy I had put down some thoughts about the Crucifixion. Now I was brooding on my own people of Scotland, a people very much preoccupied with religion and science.

For those who were sensitive, the year 1974 began with a shivering, and accelerated not so gradually into a paroxysm. It was during this year that the Arabs were thoughtless enough to at least double the price of the riches they possessed. It was really very foolish of the Pope in 1951 to banish existentialism for two reasons: first, there is no such thing as existentialism, that is, it cannot be systematized; second, it is the only view of life which holds that everything in the world is related, and in process of a relationship.

I was at this time involved with my countryman, the political economist Adam Smith, and his seminal work, *The Wealth of Nations* (1776). At one point he draws our attention to the different values put upon water and diamonds: water is necessary and cheap, and diamonds are unnecessary but dear. Now we were contemplating a situation where oil, almost as plentiful as water, certainly in the Arab countries, was being valued as rare as diamonds, certainly in economies that were just making ends meet. And of course everyone, and everything, was affected. I had had enough experience over the previous decades to draw in my horns. Curigwen and I, since the war, measured our modest economy and stuck to it.

The play weathered the storm for some months, and managed to survive the initial impact of the revolution because our initial production costs had been paid off for some time, and our cast was not all that expensive.

In my visit to West Germany with the Shakespeare company in 1950, I had noted how German trade unions had been organized into large units. Ostensibly this was easier for wage bargaining. But there was a deeper, more subtle, almost a mystical reason for this. As society was evolving towards light industry, away from heavy nineteenth-century industries, so it increased in complexity and sensitivity of technology, and at the same time became more vulnerable to any rapid or large moves in industrial relations. Movements in pay relations had to be small so that they affected large numbers without disruption.

Britain had not learned that lesson, thinking that her multiplicity of trade unions was a sign of independence and freedom. Thus, when costs rocketed due to the oil crisis, there was simply not the industrial organization to adapt to it. And our society was now so interdependent that some degree of chaos was experienced throughout.

Now that we were fortunately in Europe, having joined the EEC in 1973, we were in a much better position to find an answer. After a few months, *Lloyd George* came to an end. Then I was asked to go to South Africa with the play, but not yet, not till our autumn, their late winter. And with a new cast. Much to the pain of the family, I accepted. A new country, it would be a holiday for Curigwen; and there was apartheid. But there was more than that. Just as the horizon is peppered with clouds that gradually make their way to each other, so our lives were assuming that length of time for things like this to happen.

Curigwen had played Lyndal in an adaptation of Olive Schreiner's *Story of an African Farm* just before she joined the Old Vic company in 1939, when I first really met her. During the war I had been receiving some recruits into the army on a Saturday afternoon on the hot parade ground of Dering Lines in Brecon when a hulking fellow wearing an Anzac hat limped towards me. On my asking his name, he said 'Campbell'. 'First name?' I said. 'Roy,' he said. 'The Poet?' I said. 'Yes,' he said. I jumped up and shook him by the hand: 'How do you do, Campbell. Welcome to the British army.' His shirt had no collar, but just a bronze stud holding the ends together.

Later, after the war, meeting him outside Broadcasting House, I asked him what he was doing there. He was in the Talks Department. How? Desmond MacCarthy had published a *Sunday Times* article wondering where that South African poet was who'd written *Adamastor* and *The Flaming Terrapin*. Campbell had told him he was doorkeeper at a League of Nations office in Oxford. What the hell was he, MacCarthy, going to do about it? MacCarthy wired back saying, 'Here's five pounds, have a good dinner. Come and see me!' MacCarthy was on the BBC Committee for English. Campbell was still wearing his Anzac hat when I left him. There were too many fluxions on my South African horizon not to sample them. What about Equity? I'd been twice on the Council, and few would think I was a fellow-traveller. There were some weeks before we were to go.

During the interval the BBC asked me to do a play for them in Scotland. While I was in Glasgow, staying at the Central Hotel, I received a message from Andrew Kerr, asking if he could come to see me with some members of the Edinburgh Festival Fringe Society. I said, 'Yes, come to tea'. So he brought John Milligan, the administrator, Mike Westcott, the Vice-Chairman, and Leslie Bennie, the treasurer. And we had tea.

Then Andrew spoke. He is the Secretary, a very good lawyer, a partner in one of Edinburgh's leading law firms. The Society was founded in 1969; the first chairman was Lord Grant, a retired Scottish judge who'd just been killed in a road accident. They made no bones about it. They had tried many people before me. Would I be Chairman of the Edinburgh Festival Fringe Society? I asked a few mundane questions about organization, numbers and finance. Then I said yes. I told them that I doubted whether I would be able to attend this year's Festival, as I was contracted to go to South Africa at about the same time. They didn't mind that. They had a name to put on their paper.

We had a new cast in the play. What with rehearsals and so on, it was some weeks before I saw Soweto, the dormitory town for Black Africans who work in Johannesburg. I stood in the entrance area near the wraith of the Town Chambers, and looked westwards. Stretching away over the low hills into the horizon were long furrows of densely packed, small, grey houses, that seemed to have no end. I am not a politician, and have never belonged to any political party. I was told that over a million black Africans lived here, and the population was increasing rapidly. My eighteen months on the General Staff had been helpful. The whole world is aware of the problem of apartheid, and here I could see it before me in its particularity. If the intention was to introduce a kind of European democracy into this place, my first response was that it could not be done. No matter how well intentioned the political or religious leaders, the problem was initially one of logistics, how to establish the conditions in which democracy could exist. Not even in fifth-century Athens did Pericles believe in 'one man – one vote' – there were always qualifications.

We were living in a flat in the Maristan, near the centre of Johannesburg, within walking distance of the Academy Theatre. I usually did walk, to Curigwen's concern. The staff were black and delightful. I would encourage our black girl to talk in her dialect, and listen to the incredible pace and shape of her diction. Language begins in verse sustained by beat; but as it evolves into prose and ordinary diction, it loses the beat and slows down. I was being confronted with one of my cherished beliefs; however much I wanted the people of South Africa

115

to be individuals, they would insist on thinking tribally.

In the spring of 1939, with the Old Vic in Egypt, Curigwen and I had gone up to Luxor to see the Valley of the Kings. Looking out over the desert from the forecourt of the Luxor Palace Hotel I realized that for three thousand miles there was nothing but desert, nothing but sand between me and the Atlantic Ocean. It was from these acres of sand that thirty thousand years ago, the nomadic tribes had started their move south through the great continent. As I looked at our bubbling black girl, I seemed to detect a great hollow gap in time.

The play was doing tremendously well. Hymie Udwin, our producer, was associated in producing a native musical, *Ipi Tombi*. He told me that the musical was going to various countries to open up the world to native talent; but that when a company had gone to Australia, they couldn't endure the local life, and longed to return to the security of Soweto. I could make no moral judgements here. It was enough to try to understand.

We had become friends with Pete and Betty Suzman. We seldom talked about the political situation, but touching on the subject one day, she halted me. She told us how stunned she was when her black cook, who'd been with her for thirty years, said to her, 'You don't understand me at all, do you?'

My mind was beginning to latch on to the line of movement here. There had been in Europe in the sixteenth and seventeenth centuries two great movements of people away from political and religious persecution. One that was very familiar to us had been west from Bristol, Plymouth and other western ports across the Atlantic to the new-found continent of America. The other, from France and the Low Countries, had sailed round Spain, and south along the coast of Africa until it arrived at the Cape of Good Hope, eventually to found the city of Cape Town as a great trading post for merchants bound for the East.

After a few centuries these French and Dutch traders desired to acquire the land to their north, caring little for the native Hottentot, but eventually meeting in battle the Zulus who had taken thirty thousand years to wander south from the Sahara. Though vastly outnumbered, the whites had been triumphant, at the place called Blood River. And because of the their victory, these European settlers had deemed themselves the elect of God. Not unlike the Jews in somewhat similar circumstances, which was a little surprising, considering all things.

I did not share these thoughts with Curigwen. They usually occurred when we were lying on our backs in our bedroom, listening to a radio commentary of a rugby test between the Springboks and the British Lions. The Afrikaner accepts cricket, but rugby is his devotion. Indeed,

Curigwen had gone to Pretoria by herself to see a test match. Following the customary defeat, an Afrikaner jumped to his feet and announced passionately to the world that he would never vote for Vorster again – which, at the time, was rather like pelting the monarch with a tomato.

Yet it is an incredibly beautiful country, and was being little affected by the oil crisis. Then I remembered that South Africa, like Mycenae, was rich in gold. I met Byers Naude, a Christian, and attended meetings of groups brought together by their deep hostility to the Race Laws which separate husband from wife, and direct people to live in places where they could most easily be controlled, like Soweto.

Peggy Inglis, who was playing my wife in the play, had a small house twenty miles from Johannesburg. She invited Curigwen and me there one weekend. Night is sudden in Africa, and when it comes is very dark. Driving back to town on Sunday night, I received, I think, my most vivid memory of our visit. The only lights on the road came from the car's headlights, and every hundred yards or so they'd strike a black woman, walking on a path on the verge. Erect and tall, a figure of grace, walking with a sure step, a bundle of her possessions balanced on her head. The Afrikaner needs light; the Black African can find her way in the dark.

13 On the Fringe

After we'd finished our stint of three months in Johannesburg, we had arranged to take the play to Rhodesia (now Zimbabwe) for five weeks, visiting Bulawayo and Salisbury (now Harare). Our time in Johannesburg had really confirmed the first impression I had when looking out over the grey desert of Soweto. The problem was logistical, and would only be solved by logistics. That is, a massive injection of capital was needed for building and education so that a new environment might be created, suitable for the practice of modern democracy – which depended, more than at any other time, on the concept of the individual.

The concept of the individual, as I now saw it, had become essential with the inroads science was making on political and religious analysis. From physics came the insights of Einstein and Clerk Maxwell, and from biology the consequences of genetic evolution.

The difference existing between South Africa and Rhodesia was immediately noticeable – in a lowering of tension. Round the centre of Johannesburg were high buildings, looking down on a closed-in lake. In Bulawayo, the streets are wide; what did it matter if they were created so that bullock-drawn carts could turn round in them? The impression they gave now was one of openness to a wide, high sky.

In South Africa, the beautiful land with its secret wealth was a source of division. Here in Rhodesia, the rich, overt crops invited harmony between the races. And so I could go on, drawing contrasts between the two disparate parts of southern Africa.

In the seventies in South Africa, due to the increase in technology in all aspects of commercial life, the gap between the two races would

118

increase, emphasizing the lack of understanding expressed by Betty Suzman's cook. In Rhodesia, the country was lightly industrialized, and less densely populated, encouraging a gentle approach between the two communities. Again, in religion, which was Christianity on both sides, there was a contrast. In South Africa, it issued in an extreme fundamentalism, while, in Rhodesia, pressures relaxed into a benevolent Anglicanism. It was not surprising that the Rhodesian problem would be solved. It is not surprising that the South African problem remains, and its solution will emerge unpredictably.

As far as I was concerned, what was emerging from our visit to these two countries at this particular time was that I was using my imagination in an independent way. No doubt my mind and my memory were involved as part of the inseparable trinity of mind, but the evidence that was being presented to the trinity, I felt, came exclusively from my imagination. While I was familiar with the situation, it was my imagination that enabled me to distance myself from it.

We had a few days off, and we went to the Victoria Falls. Even nature has its off days, and though the Zambezi was not in full spate the Falls were impressive enough. But it was not the Falls for which I will remember this place. On the road to the Falls there stands the statue of a man, one foot forward, in nineteenth-century explorer's uniform, peering out over the Falls. There is a name on it – it is David Livingstone; under it, a date – it is 1855. It was not my mind that raced, it was not my memory, for it had never been here before. It was my imagination that was leaping beyond all the barriers. In 1855, Livingstone was the first white man to look over the Zambezi, and that was then only a hundred and twenty years ago. Everything that had happened in Rhodesia had happened in that brief space of time. 1855 – that was seven years after Marx and Engels had issued the Communist Manifesto in Paris. 1855 – that was four years before the publication of *The Origin of Species*, and Darwin knew nothing of the land that Livingstone was overlooking for the first time. And my imagination was telling me all this. Not the imagination that is supposed to be the home of fantasy, but the real imagination which lies outside the mind and the memory, and assembles its own library of facts to fertilize the activities of the mind and the memory. And Livingstone was a Scotsman. He must have his place in the *Bedside Book* – the thought of that book reared before me, inviting me to go home. We did.

The 1974 Edinburgh Festival passed in my absence. When we returned,

119

I took up my post as Chairman of the Edinburgh Festival Fringe Society. This meant travelling to Edinburgh every month, more or less, for directors' meetings. It soon became clear to me that I was presiding over one of the most efficient organizations in the British theatre. With Andrew Kerr for legal matters on my left, Leslie Bennie for financial matters on my right; at the other end of the table, Mike Westcott, the vice-chairman, sitting with John Milligan, the admistrator; the other directors filling in the gaps. They had assured me that it would not be onerous; nor was it. What they did not know about me was my interest in technique.

The Festival started in 1947 at the prompting of Rudolph Bing (whom I had known in the Company of Four days), and the then Lord Provost. The second Festival saw the Guthrie production of *The Thrie Estaites*, the play I told Tony I didn't understand. The third Festival elicited from Robert Kemp, a journalist friend of mine, a note in the *Edinburgh Evening News* that 'the usual fringe' would be there. So, in the best organic way, a growth evolved.

The fifties and sixties was the time when our universities exploded, especially after the Robbins Report, pouring out students from the Arts departments for whom Edinburgh and its fringe had all the attractions and delight of freedom for a prisoner liberated from the gulag. Prominent among these participating almost from the beginning were students from the mostly ancient colleges of Oxford and Cambridge; and it was their voice really in the sixties, when young people were flocking to it, who insisted on a proper organization being formed. This happened in 1969, with Lord Grant as chairman. It was his sudden death in a road accident that caused the vacancy that the committee had such difficulty in filling before they asked me.

Robin Midgley asked me soon after our return if I would do *Lloyd George Knew My Father* for the last time at the Haymarket Theatre, Leicester, where he was the director. Fortunately I did, though I was becoming increasingly busy with the *Scottish Bedside Book* after Livingstone, attracted more by the achievements of one who was to preoccupy my spare time almost more than any other, James Clerk Maxwell. My interest here started with some words by Einstein in a centenary tribute to Maxwell: 'Since Maxwell's time, Physical Reality has been thought of as represented by continuous fields, governed by partial differential equations, and not capable of any mechanical interpretation. This change in the conception of Reality is the most profound and the most fruitful that physics has experienced since the time of Newton.' This was before I had discovered Maxwell's teasing correspondence with Faraday.

120

While I was playing at Leicester, Robin quite suddenly asked me whether there was anything I wanted to do. I looked at him for some time. Then I said, 'Do you know Ibsen's last play, *When We Dead Awaken*?' He had not read it. Three days later he asked me whether I would do it at Leicester. This was spring 1975. Not till the autumn, I said. There was the Edinburgh Festival for which I had written an experimental play, *Games* (this was tried out at the studio theatre, before going on to Edinburgh), and I needed time to learn the part, which was a long one. He agreed. My year was now planned. Any gaps were filled by the *Bedside Book*, which was now taking shape.

And so to Edinburgh. Why did I find the Fringe so exhilarating? It was not the performances, but the number of women who would stop me in the street and glare at me: 'Why,' they would say, 'do you allow such things to happen?' Usually they were referring to some young student who had conceived a new idea of mime which involved his standing in the middle of the stage, staring at the audience, slowly undressing himself, and announcing, 'Time is passing.'

I could not really explain what it was all about – at least, not what the young people were doing and why. I could explain what I was doing, and why this extraordinary event was taking place at Edinburgh. That was the simplest bit. Of all the cities in Europe, Edinburgh, with its abundant churches, halls and spaces inherited from the Reformation and the Enlightenment, could provide a variety of stages suitable for every kind of entertainment from a monologue on James Joyce to a school from England providing a musical of its own contriving. The Fringe was the first example of a new kind of openness.

And it was not like Avignon, the only other city in Europe at the time engaged in this sort of enterprise. Edinburgh was concentrated into a few square miles. Running through it like a spine was a Royal Mile, beginning, like Athens, on a great rock, and running down to a palace in a great park. There were three reasons for its growth. The first was the vast number of students pouring out of the unversities and colleges of technology or education that had no public stage to present themselves.

The second was that the third revolution in the theatre begun by Ibsen was being absorbed and nothing new was appearing on the horizon. It was therefore a time of experiment. The Communists' socialist realism, Brecht's epic theatre, Claudel's total theatre did not satisfy that immediacy with depth which the players and audience were seeking, a search for a new kind of identity and authenticity. I found it heartening that, whatever the quality of the performance, there were always in the programme small groups exploring the writers and artists

121

of the great period at the turn of the century. Small plays on T. S. Eliot, James Joyce, D. H. Lawrence, mixed in with Beckett and Pinter, out of which would emerge a new sensibility, a new kind of experience.

But the third and most important reason for the growth was economic. Costs in every department were limiting enterprise and stifling imagination. In the professional theatre I could see the general tendency to repetition, to repeat the successful past, to play safe in spite of the changing climate towards, paradoxically, a wholeness that was continually in movement. The Festival Fringe Society solved, for those who wished to participate, problems of rent, rates, maintenance, by encouraging the people of Edinburgh to hire out their spaces, and with them all the technical matters, like publicity, box office, local regulations and so on. In short, nature had provided the idea, the Fringe Society provided the technique, and the participating groups provided the energy. With such insights, fifth-century Athens created the first glimpse of civilization.

The burden of innovation lay with the Administrator, and it was my job as Chairman to encourage anything that would increase the technical expertness of the groups. From early on, the *Scotsman*, the local daily newspaper, without prompting, bodied forth the policy by devoting an enormous amount of space to reviews. All the time it is increasing in professionalism; and the innovations have been quite startling.

The invitation to play Rubek in *When We Dead Awaken* (1899), Ibsen's last play, at Leicester made me pause. I felt I had to review my thoughts about acting in the light of how I'd moved since last playing Solness, which was indeed brief but had somehow collected my thoughts, particularly on how an actor saw the mind, the memory and the imagination, and the new view of time. My daughter Marty had been at the Drama Centre, London where acting seemed to be taught as a mystery, a hermetic craft available only to the initiated. I was outside reception of this message.

Again, Stanislavsky had used an approach to producing Chekhov, generally called the 'Method', which had spawned new directions in acting from the Actors Studio in New York to Saint-Denis in England. Ibsen and Chekhov were in drama the carriers of the new sensibility of the twentieth century that had been opened up by Darwin and Einstein. Their messages were conveyed in texts, in a new language, in a new range of characters. In a new kind of society that was moving inward, where the 'what' of objects was giving way to the 'how' of people. In

An Actor Prepares, Stanislavsky had stimulated me to much thought. He writes:

> 'When the inner world of someone you have under observation becomes clear to you through his acts, thoughts and impulses, follow his actions closely and study the conditions in which he finds himself. Why did he do this or that? What did he have in mind?
>
> 'Very often we cannot come through definite data to know the inner life of the person we are studying, and can only reach towards it by means of intuitive feeling. Here we are dealing with the most delicate type of concentration of attention, and with powers of observation that are subconscious in their origin. Our ordinary type of attention is not sufficiently far-reaching to carry out the process of penetrating another person's soul.
>
> 'If I were to assure you that your technique could achieve so much I should be deceiving you. As you progress you will learn more and more ways in which to stimulate your subconscious selves, and to draw them into your creative process, but it must be admitted that we cannot reduce this study of the inner life of other human beings to a scientific technique.'

There were few, if any, directors of his time in Europe who could have written with such clarity of the direction acting must go. It was my exploration of subjectivity in acting that had first excited me in Kierkegaard, and secondly in setting before myself, as a measure of my professional life, acting in Ibsen's plays. Like the Danish critic Georg Brandes, but for very different reasons, I had realized a kind of complementarity between Ibsen and Kierkegaard. With some irony, I saw it as one of the first examples of the new dispensation in space, of bodies acting on each other at a distance. What was flying between the two? Could it be offence, that which had preoccupied me so much at the Savoy Theatre during the run of *Alibi*? Kierkegaard suggests in *The Sickness unto Death*: 'But offence is the most decisive determinant of subjectivity, of the individual man, the most decisive it is possible to think of – even thought must admit that offence even more than love is an unreal concept which only becomes real when there is an individual who is offended by the self.'

It is offence that in *The Wild Duck* drives Hedvig into old Ekdal's attic, causes Hedda Gabler to withdraw behind the curtain, makes Solness the Master Builder climb the tower, all to their hidden deaths. The notion of offence was enormously important, not only for Ibsen's plays, but in a society increasingly aware of freedom. I think it was Ibsen's task to give particularity to this general sense. My reason for studying *When We Dead Awaken* for many hours was twofold. First, I distrusted the overt reasons for his range of symbols in the play, wrapped round words like 'soul', 'creation', 'resurrection' and so on; secondly, his melodramatic stage directions, while entirely in accordance with nineteenth-century custom, introduced a rhetoric at odds with the inward relationship of Rubek and Irene. Inwardness cannot be openly expressed. It is an indirect experience, revealed, at least dramatically in Ibsen's plays, through mockery and wonder, despair and vanity, riding on a basic passionate intentness between the characters.

Thus, while love is primarily understood as a physical relationship between two characters, it is when it expands through time and experience that the possibility of incompatibility occurs. With incompatibility the individual self is offended, and then offence turns back on itself in true love, or explodes into immediacy, usually with catastrophic results. *When We Dead Awaken* traces the incompatibility between two people until love turns back on itself, and dissolves the offence, yet ends in death because it cannot be sustained. That one of the characters, Rubek, is a sculptor suggests that the play is largely autobiographical. While the counterpoint to the heart-searching of the main characters is provided by a brazen sensuality between Rubek's young wife and Ulfheim, a hunter.

Robin Midgley phoned me during the Edinburgh Festival to say he couldn't direct the play himself, but Michael Meacham would do it. Renee Asherson played Irene, and Heather Sears was Maja. The theatre had bought a screen on which were back-projected wonderful slides of Norwegian fjords. No one noticed it. But I found it a great experience.

To some extent, when I played Rubek I thought that my measure as an actor was complete, in that, getting on, I would not have the energy for a major part. So it was good that I could turn to the *Bedside Book* and Jenny Carter. Behind all my work in the theatre, I was burrowing away in the London Library, gradually filling in the pattern of the *Bedside Book*. I would select these extracts, have them copied, send them to Jenny in Scotland. She would then make the necessary contacts so that I could use them.

In one year I had observed the technique of openness being practised at the fringe of the Edinburgh Festival, providing, so I thought, a pattern of a new kind of organization in society, in how to encourage people to come together from the roots up, instead of being dictated to from above. And then, in the play, I had explored the layers of sensibility between two unique individuals, in the present moment in time. Openness was clearly being understood in our society, as witness the reaction to closed and hidden restrictions. But the consequences for thought of Crick and Watson's gene were not nearly so widely understood. That every individual on earth is absolutely unique was a big cherry to bite. Yet its implications for politics were beginning to be understood. But the neurophysiolgist still persevered in his efforts to find in the brain the source of the mind. I was now convinced that if we were all different, this distinction showed only in the mind, the memory, and the imagination, and was primarily revealed through art.

The play had shown incompatibility and offence experienced between two characters. But the same elements were present in the relations between nations. Indeed very immediately, as I saw, between Scotland and England. The biggest burden to change in nations in the twentieth century is the failure to adapt to light and communications. When change in these elements is not harmonious, then incompatibility and offence occur, as they have between Scotland and England. Scotland was slow to loosen its heavy industrial inheritance from the nineteenth century, and the diversity of communications with its impact on communicable language encouraged a withdrawal into insularity.

The *Bedside Book* was an opportunity to recall men of some significance who had altered not merely Scots views but world views. The three obvious choices were Adam Smith, the philosopher David Hume and Clerk Maxwell. The Scottish popular novelist John Buchan suggests that every Scotsman is born a metaphysician, which was all very well at the time Buchan was writing, before philosophy had disintegrated. What struck me about the great period of Scottish history, which lasts for one hundred and fifty years from 1750 to 1900, was, first of all, its astonishingly rapid recovery from the failure of the Jacobite wars, and then its amazing diversity. The philosophy of existence is grounded in the view that everything relates. If so, then the great thinkers of these years were masters in spreading their energies over the interrelationship of modes of thought and existence. Reading Adam Smith, I found that subsequent great economists like David Ricardo, J. M. Keynes and Marx had not dimmed his perceptions of what makes a nation's wealth. Hume I found the example of a complete man, bounden only to his own truth.

14 Science into Words

Maxwell's significance emerges fully only when he is held in the mind with Faraday. Together, they provide a partial suggestion of a new approach to reality as seen by a supremely gifted empirical scientist, Faraday, and one of the world's greatest mathematicians, Maxwell, who, like Newton, was a great experimenter and humanist. Together, they throw a blinding light on a fundamental question that surrounds all scientific work; can science be put into words? While I was reading about Maxwell I came on a letter Faraday, aged sixty-six, wrote in 1857 to Maxwell, aged twenty-six:

> There is one thing I would be glad to ask you. When a
> mathematician engaged in investigating physical actions and
> results has arrived at his conclusions, may they not be expressed
> in common language as fully, clearly, and definitely as in
> mathematical formulae? If so, would it not be a great boon to
> such as we to express them so? translating them out of their
> hieroglyphics, that we might also work on them, by experiment.
> I think it must be so.

Behind all my work in the theatre and my reading in science, there had lurked a question: how could an actor contribute to the problem of putting science into words? Reading Sherrington had started me by his amazing description of the eye, and the extraordinary, detailed differentials in its construction. Light reached the brain by way of the eye. Again, in his Gifford lectures on man's nature, he excluded, in his description of the nervous system, any consideration of the mind, the

126

memory and the imagination, holding them to be not suitable for scientific description.

My feelings, then, in these years after the war, Watson's *The Double Helix* was not published until 1968, was that if genetic difference signalled the uniqueness of individuals, a similar difference was observable in the individual mind, something we had only grasped tentatively, if at all, through the artefacts of art. To discover a request by Faraday on a matter which had engaged me greatly was of special importance, coming as it did from a great intuitive scientist with little mathematics. I was now engaged in a new kind of thriller of my own contriving.

At Edinburgh, Maxwell had had the traditional Scottish education, beginning with Greek and Latin, and extending beyond mathematics into metaphysics, logic and other humanities. It was out of this background that he recognized that the mathematical problems of Faraday's lines of force (which he could solve) also raised problems in the field of philosophy, of understanding. I have come to see that while Maxwell's scientific discoveries, and his equations, were vital in Einstein's leap into space-time, it is his solutions to Faraday's question of putting his science into words that become enormously significant. I, as an actor, began to feel a wonderful empathy with Maxwell.

Maxwell's solution to the problem of understanding the working of electricity and magnetism was that we must use analogy. In his paper 'On Faraday's Lines of Force' he says: 'In order to obtain physical ideas without adopting a physical theory, we must make ourselves familiar with the existence of physical analogies. By a physical analogy I mean that partial similarity between the laws of one science and those of another which makes each of them illustrate the other.' And he finishes: 'The only laws of nature are those which our minds must fabricate, and the only laws of mind are fabricated for it by matter.'

In the London Library, while waiting for my books, I stood near a shelf containing books just returned. Looking at these one day, I saw one with the title *The Making of Homeric Verse* by Milman Parry.

Milman Parry was a Welsh-American professor of Greek at a university in California. A young man like Ventris, he loved Greece and had the intellectual gifts to exercise his analysis on the first great epics of civilization, the *Iliad* and the *Odyssey*. Like Ventris, he died early, in a gun accident, but not before he'd completed his Greek studies. It is the characteristic of all academics, and this applied to Parry, to proliferate examples. This is the result of an increasing dependence in all quarters on statistics. However, when I had worked through his book, dominated by the study of language and the line of Homeric verse, I had extracted two themes which at this time resonated through my mind. The first

127

was the noun-epithet and verb formula of the Greek line, that is the Greek line in the epics moves from the subject to the object, in contrast to the Latin line which moves from the object to the subject; thereby making it enormously difficult for the early Latinists to translate and transform the New Testament.

But it was Parry's second conclusion that riveted me, his conviction that the epics could only be understood as an analogy. They were like the events of the Trojan War, but not the thing itself, reality at one remove. This I could well understand, having seen the ruins of Troy and the drowsy Scamander. But the idea of analogy set alight the three notions that had intermittently occupied my thoughts for years: the nature of the mind, the memory and the imagination. For while the Homeric poets were near enough to the event to recall it, the terms in which they related it were so rich, diverse, human and even extravagant that it could be said in their creation they had discovered a new dimension of mind, that could only have been released under the rubric of analogy. That was imagination. And looking back at the great variations of metre that the Greek dramatists had discovered, I could now subsume them under the general term 'analogy'. Grammarians could spend their lives ferreting out the differences. Clearly, Maxwell and Parry had opened windows into my mind.

I was still doing odd things for television, still encouraging the administrators of the Festival Fringe to improve our technique. The children had now asserted their differences. All had left home. One was even married and beginning her own family. My *Bedside Book* was published. Silence! For most of the decade I had been preoccupied by the book. I was tolerably well known from my various activities. Yet, it did not even provoke resentment, which I would have enjoyed greatly.

Then St Andrew's University informed me that I was to be honoured with a doctorate of laws (D.Litt.). It was very moving. Years earlier, I had received a letter in the strictest confidence from the Prime Minister suggesting something similar, but I told him in the strictest confidence not to proceed. Then my position as a rogue and vagabond would have been jeopardized, since it was part of my anonymity in measuring my life. The day that Henry Irving accepted his knighthood was a disaster for English actors, it robbed their craft of mystery, and seriousness.

Now I went to St Andrews with Curigwen to receive my degree, assured in my mind that those who noticed would be full of wonder at such an event. That would be the proper response. The day of the ceremony was beautiful, and we were to assemble in the morning in the vestry of the university church for a service of thanksgiving. We arrived early, and were shown to an empty vestry. I thought the staff a trifle lax in their duties. I was certain of this when two other people were shown into the vestry, both French.

My mind, with that rapidity which it always shows on these occasions, recalled an episode in 1939 with Curigwen: when returning to Athens from Delphi, our bus broke down. We were to open in the National theatre that night in *The Rivals*. The plain and the road were very deserted, then suddenly a car emerged in the distance. I dashed towards it, and waved it to stop. I opened the car door, and very breathlessly I said, 'Parlare Inglese?' A very elegant, elderly man sitting in the corner said, 'Yes, I speak English.' I was so anxious that I didn't even notice how foolish I had been. But I explained the problem. He understood. His name was Rodocanachi. He knew London well. Would we join him and be his guests at a restaurant in Thebes, where he heard the red mullet was excellent?

After lunch we had got on so splendidly that our host with a great half-moon smile on his face turned to me and said, 'You know, yours is the worst Italian I've ever heard spoken,' and he roared with laughter. I giggled a little at what I might have said, but I didn't: 'I know, and you have been misinformed, your red mullet isn't so wonderful!'

For a moment I thought of speaking my worst French to the two visitors. Then the door burst open, and Lord Ballantrae entered in full sail, a monocle in his eye, at which my heart, with rapidity, sank only to recover the next moment when I heard him burst into perfect French. Then, turning to me, he said, 'Mr Cruickshank, this is Fernand Braudel, who is receiving a degree with you.' The world is not a small place. It is wonderfully large, where the miraculous sometimes happens.

Meeting Braudel had brought his great work, *The Mediterranean . . .*, before me. It had reared up like an angry stallion, daring me to go his way. It was too vast, too detailed, yet its direction was right. It was at the same time deep and vertical, expressing a confused complexity that had always been evident since the cave drawings at Lascaux. It was so much easier to disregard this complexity and relax in the company of great men, or suffer vicariously. Let someone else do the suffering – it was a pleasure to enjoy the spectacle. A new kind of understanding was being forced on us.

Refusing an honour from a Prime Minister had been right. I wished to retain my position as an actor, not as a social object. Now that I was a D.Litt., I had given a kind of warning to those who were sensitive that I was engaged in an enterprise that, arising out of the theatre, looked beyond it, and yet was experienced at its clearest in the theatre. And after Clark Maxwell, in the experience of television which Clerk Maxwell's equations had done so much to create. We should always compare upwards. Scotland had treated him abominably. It had preferred William Thomson: the country had made him a peer as Lord Kelvin, the city of Glasgow had dubbed many of its thoroughfares with his name. Maxwell's home in Galloway is today a gaping ruin, the home once of one of the three great creators of the modern world. I was getting on, but I vowed to myself to dedicate my waning energies to him. I hoped I would be spared the time.

What did Maxwell and Milman Parry in their own fields mean by analogy? I felt this was the beginning I must make – even as an actor. What was the difference between identity and analogy? To understand Maxwell on this was necessary not merely to the understanding of his science, since his comments (for the benefit of Faraday, who had more mathematics than me) spread over the whole field of human understanding. As I had found, following Milman Parry, Maxwell says: 'That analogies appear to exist is plain in the face of things, for all parables, fables, similes, metaphors, tropes and figures of speech are analogies, natural or revealed, artificial or concealed.... Neither is there any question as to the occurrence of analogies to our minds. They are as plenty as reasons, not to say blackberries.'

What started me on this absurd search on how to equate Maxwell's equations with the field of my own mind and memory and imagination was Sherrington's work on the nervous system in *Man and his Nature* and the speed of light in Einstein's notable equation. In the nervous system, at no time does the speed of an impulse exceed 100 metres per second, whereas in Einstein's equation light moves at 186,000 miles per second, the upper limit of time. Finally, light, like the mind, is always 'now'. Even when the mind is thinking about the past, it is always in the present.

There was a kind of consolation in all this. I had come to be unhappy with the notion of cause and affect, so that thinking abstractly about forces that had no weight and were invisible had the attraction of novelty and the absurd. That the universe was never at rest, and consequently we were not only constantly on the move but leaning on a curve, was a new kind of excitement. The confrontation between science and art, far from being a fight over ultimate truth and reality, became for me a marriage of analogies and a desperate fight to keep things separate, so that my family would not call me a mixed-up kid.

To prove an insight, scientists repeat experiments until by sheer repetition and the weight of statistics their experiment ceases to be a probability and becomes a fact. How on earth could I in my situation as an actor find an incident that would prove the equation of my mind, memory and imagination as a field analagous to Maxwell's electromagnetic field? I started with one advantage. As far as our minds, memories, and imaginations are concerned, they might as well be abstract, as no one can see them. Nor can anyone see the operation of Maxwell's equations.

15 At the National Theatre

I was interrupted in my thoughts on Maxwell by a summons to the National Theatre to meet Edward Bond. Bond had been much involved at the Royal Court, a theatre that like the National, had until now, existed on my periphery; the conjunction of Bond and the National was intriguing. I had by now perfected that direct, intent look which, accompanied by silence, doctors turn on patients to petrify them with uncertainty; only I used it as a prelude to wonder. When I heard what Bond and Gillian Diamond, the casting authority, had in store for me, I turned this gaze on them. It was really absurd. The Greeks were at it again. They wanted me to play Nestor in a play, *The Woman*, written, and to be directed, by Bond.

All true dramatists feel that at some time in their career they must come to terms with Athens and the Greek dramatists. Usually it is through a single play. Racine reinvents Euripides' Hippolytus in seventeenth-century France; Eliot transforms the third play of Aeschylus' trilogy, *The Eumenides*, into *The Family Reunion*; the only time I'd played Agamemnon was in André Obey's *Sacrifice to the Wind*, an adaptation of Euripides' *Iphigenia in Aulis*. But Bond, if a communist, was very independent. It was as though he had observed the scene of Troy and the situation at the time in Athens, listened to the voices coming from Mycenae and Thebes through the families of Agamemnon and Oedipus, glanced at Troilus and Cressida, laid all the bits out on a table, then with an eye on Brecht, picked out the characters that had had least attention and stirred them into a first-class piece of epic theatre. So Hecuba, Ismene, Cassandra and Nestor were elevated into the limelight, Ismene adopting the incarceration of Antigone, all given modern reference by a dark man who has escaped from the silver mines of Athens. Bond's invention and writing were vivid and his production exciting; it was a much better play than he was given credit for. But then we are no longer tutored in Greek. I was seventy and the challenge to my energy very exhilarating.

After the play had opened, I had a few days off so I went up to Edinburgh, where the Festival had started. While I was there, they phoned me from the National to say that their next production was John Galsworthy's *Strife* (1909) and they wanted me to play John Anthony, the protagonist of capitalism in the play, with Christopher Morahan directing. Again it was to be produced in the Olivier Theatre – I had come to love the vast spaces of the place. There was a continual invitation to rival a piece of Greek statuary in relation to the almost semi-circled audience, and its size always threatened to swallow one's voice. In short, its ambience was a constant temptation to one's mind to see the plays in a space–time continuum; the very reverse of the intimacy I was commending for the small places at Edinburgh. I felt that these extremes provided for the modern actor the range of limits in which we must become expert in our diverse world.

The situation in *Strife* was a reflection of what was happening off-stage at the National itself, where the management were in conflict with some members of the stage staff – about money. It was typical of the state into which labour relations had fallen, in contrast with those of Germany. A small group could assert its rights even to the extent of calling a strike and crippling a production because it held the maintenance of its rights superior to a loyalty of relationship. Some stagehands had over the years so increased their salaries through the threatening of strikes that a level had been reached beyond which it was impossible to go. But they insisted and, with some irony, the strike occurred at the opening of the play dealing with a precisely similar subject. The play was unnoticed; and I should have felt bitter, because I was very happy playing the capitalist. The actors insisted on the play going on, despite the braziers of the pickets round the theatre, with the strikers stamping their feet and blowing their hands in a mock show of picketry (all of them were earning much more than the actors).

In Germany, trade unions were limited to what was essential, and demands were pitched at a modest degree, aware that excessive claims would play havoc in an interrelated society, as all Western societies were becoming under the pressure of light-orientated industry. But in Britain, trade unions still brandished a specious identity to sustain their

133

differentials, irrespective of the suffering it might cause to those around them. I had little sympathy with the strikers, and was glad when the play finished, especially as it was to be replaced by a play about Mozart, Peter Shaffer's *Amadeus*, in which Peter Hall invited me to participate modestly. As Count Orsini-Rosenberg, I was given the most comic line in the play, ('Too many notes,' as a comment on Mozart's music) and the painful duty of destroying a Mozart manuscript.

I was by now becoming accustomed to the atmosphere of the National Theatre. Normally, theatres acquire a singular identity in relation to the surroundings in which they find themselves, and in conjunction with their owners put on a shape and colour which mark their individuality. I could not find any such distinction at the National; it was as though the building were indifferent. As well it might be, since it was the equivalent in contemporary terms of theatre to what a factory was in industrial terms. I felt this very much during the production period of the play.

The two plays I'd already been in had started with accepted texts, and proceeded normally. Not so with *Amadeus*. Shaffer was a distinguished dramatist; apart from his successful West End plays, he had been done at the Old Vic. He straddled the whole world of theatre. It was all the more surprising that after the first read-through, and as we began rehearsing – eight weeks at least – the rehearsals were interrupted by Shaffer. He is not a tall man, and looked like a demented accountant who has lost an invoice, appearing with a sheaf of notes in his hand. These were apparently rewrites, which he delivered to the appointed actor – rather like Amphitryon selecting Zeus's victims. Those actors who received no notes goggled enviously. After a few rehearsals, Paul Scofield, who was playing Mozart's rival, Antonio Salieri, and was embedded in a wheelchair as though he had never known anything else, would receive his impassively. It took me a little time to realize that this was Shaffer's technique; and while it was a trifle difficult to get some idea of the shape of the play, Shaffer and Peter Hall knew what they were doing.

One day I was walking down the long corridor to Rehearsal Room Four with Hall. Looking down at me, he said that he'd had supper the previous night with Trevor Nunn and Peter Brook, old chums of his. I murmured something, and smiled at the word 'chums'. 'Yes', he said. 'We meet every now and then to have a look over the London theatre.' I looked at him, and he smiled. We were at the rehearsal room. What had the man meant? Was he suggesting a Roman triumvirate in the process of dividing the spoils? For a moment I was perturbed and the thought flashed through my mind of the openness of the Edinburgh Fringe.

Hall's oblique words indicated something that the indifference of the building induced – uncertainty. Sometimes members of the cast disappeared, and it transpired on their return that they had climbed the Jacob's ladder from the bowels of the rehearsal room to the casting office on the fourth floor. There would then be a hurried discussion of what programme the management had in mind, who was in and who was out. The rehearsals were a mixture of present fluxion and future probability. Occasionally Hall would play a record of the *Lacrimosa* to remind us that we were rehearsing a play about Mozart.

Wilfully or otherwise, Shaffer had stumbled on a magnificent subject for the theatre. The life and genius of Mozart intertwined with the ambiguous interest and envy of Salieri, in a courtly atmosphere completely unable to appreciate the novelty of Mozart, ending in his unpredictable death with the Requiem Mass unfinished, his bones emptied out into oblivion. The whole thing was an enterprise in which I could bring Mozart and Maxwell together. I had inherited a dressing room from Elizabeth Spriggs, who very kindly left her divan for my comfort. This cell was ideal for the technique I had used on the previous occasions when I had been in long runs in the theatre: to set myself a task of immediate relevance yet of general significance. Mozart's mind must be my objective. Maxwell's equations, the stepping stones.

I found my age of great advantage. When I was a boy, my parents had bought me a crystal set which I used to listen to in my bed at night in the dark, transported to the Piccadilly or Savoy hotels to hear the De Groot or Carroll Gibbons orchestras, or an epilogue in a strange English voice. Then in my mid-teens when I had started singing, I broadcast from 2BD, the Aberdeen station of the BBC in Belmont Street. I think I was the first to broadcast Milne's *When We Were Very Young*. This must have been in the year 1925.

Once in the theatre, it took some time to break into the BBC. But television had started and in 1937 I broadcast with Olivier in an extract from *Macbeth*. All this was due to the discovery by Faraday of the electro-magnetic lines of force, the fields of Maxwell's equations, a new universe of fields, abstract and sub-atomic.

But the most significant fact emerging from this history was Maxwell's use in his equations of light, light moving at 186,000 miles per second. Light that entered my eye at the same speed, the 'now' of Maxwell's

135

equations matching my mind, memory and imagination. But how could it be proved? Just as the web of ambition, envy, frustration, hope and energy in the theatre forced me to retreat into my dressing room, once in my cell another web of numbers, ideas, fields, confused me. I must escape into Mozart. Certain facts about him fascinated me. From the beginning his imagination was first rate; his work was accomplished in a remarkably short time, his energy was great and varied. He could concentrate on a game of billiards as intensely as on a symphony. Even though his last illness was final, it was his body that died; his mind was working up to the last minute of his body's defeat, leaving the Requiem unfinished.

There was one moment in the play when we were all listening to the first performance of *The Marriage of Figaro*; only that part in the fourth act where the reconciliation between the Count and Countess occurs was used. The beauty of the phrase never palled on me, and every night of the performance I would ask myself, 'How did Mozart do it?' What was the nature of his mind? One of the advantages of being in a play like *Amadeus*, about one of the great artists of all times, was that it raised the point about art. This had been a belief of mine since the war, that art was the solution to problems that could not be solved in any other way. What was the problem here? Mozart's mind, of course. Still brooding on analogy, I came on a phrase of Maxwell, that his equations should be regarded as illustrative, not explanatory. Wasn't this the thing about Mozart? He wasn't explaining anything. His illustrations were always beautiful. I must persevere with Maxwell; I might find something analogous. Sometimes I'd roar in laughter at myself, peering into the mirror. I considered myself extremely lucky.

I don't think I could have continued my reflection and reading if my life at this time had been anything but a calm repetition and a modest, controlled motion. We live in Victoria; and with my senior citizen's pass I would daily, somewhat like the fixed routine of the philosopher Immanuel Kant in Koenigsberg, make my way by bus to Waterloo, then through the pedestrian tunnels and sunken pedestrian square of grafitti to the theatre. Curigwen and I were alone. The family was evolving autonomously. Our days were passed in gentle pleasure. And always the call of my cell at the National which I had to smother, it threatened to envelop me. And then it happened.

It occurs in a book by R. A. R. Tricker and it is about Faraday and Maxwell's contribution to science; the remark is ultimately due to Lewis Carroll, also (as C. L. Dodgson) a mathematician. Tricker notes that Maxwell, in his paper *A Dynamical Theory of the Electromagnetic Field*, cuts out the complicated structure of elastic vortices and idle wheels (as well he might, they were abstract), and leaves only the essential mathematical theory. And then comes the crucial comment: he likens this to Alice's Cheshire cat, when the cat vanishes, but the grin remains. The cat vanishes, but the grin remains. As I listened to the Count's dying fall that night, a great feeling of peace came over me. There was the music, and the music of Mozart. Nothing else was required. And was not this the solution to all art, the grin that remains because it is always now, and the observer's mind is always now? Silently I roared. I had seen Maxwell's equation in the beauty of Mozart. Mozart's beauty was unique because the equations of his mind were unique. Just as our genes were unique, so were our equations. I had to grin. How could I prove it? My theory was a theory that I could only prove by myself. But how?

Once I had tied up the equations with the field of the mind, I began to see them everywhere, in my colleagues, in the plays I was asked to do. But I daren't say anything about it. Who on earth would believe me if I told them that their minds were really empty sub-atomic fields, the spaces round objects that were held in a kind of tension of electromagnetic phenomena whose changes in time and space lead to electrical and magnetic forces but that the fields could not be seen or measured? Maxwell's equations did not explain the forces; what they did was to reflect the massive potential of variety if, as I now believed, they were an analogy for the human mind.

What was driving me was a conviction to the depth of my being that the crowd was untruth! All my life I'd endured with others the attempt of groups to impose their ideas on me. This revulsion crystallized round the prewar German cry, 'Sieg Heil'. Heard from the crowd at a Nuremberg rally, my memory can still burn me with it. So it was as a Russian peasant in Leo Tolstoy's *The Fruits of Enlightenment* (1891) I could, while waiting in the kitchen for food, wonder about the delay before new ideas are accepted.

Or while cavorting round a hilly slope during a picnic in Alan Ayckbourn's *Sisterly Feelings*, I would brood on the matter of grace and style as my young colleagues presented it in their vivid youth. With Shakespeare, my thoughts were easy: in *As You Like It* there was the ages of man, the equations of the mind as they are reflected in the changing body; and in *Richard III*, to recollect playing Brackenbury watching the Hastings of Gielgud, aeons ago.

With Brecht's *The Life of Galileo* my thoughts were more relevant, because I was now verging on the new world that I had to define. I had a modest part at the beginning of the play and could have gone home but such was my feeling for Galileo, and Michael Gambon played

137

the part superbly, I always stayed for the curtain. Perhaps it was because we had absorbed all Brecht's notions about alienation and the like, but the play seemed in a perfectly normal historical tradition. The subject, however, made it different. Here, Maxwell reasserted himself. And, after a long time, Kierkegaard.

Following Copernicus and Galileo, our understanding of the world was beginning to change. It was not merely that the world was continually in movement, continually dynamic, but also that society had failed to see how ideas and structures must change in the light of the new discoveries in physics and biology which had reached their climax in the first half of the twentieth century.

And yet it was not so simple. I had been riding a tandem and had not noticed it. For one thing, the mind that drew the horse at Lascaux was exactly like mine, even though some ten thousand years separated us. Given my understanding of the mind in the twentieth century as an analogy of Maxwell's equations, there is no way in which the fundamental components the mind, the memory and the imagination could have evolved in any Darwinian sense. But given Maxwell's equations, an enormous expansion of individual minds became possible. Indeed, I could see little evolution of mind compared with the massive increase in our knowledge and understanding of the physical universe, that which lay outside the mind, in the last ten millennia. That our imaginations and memories had created structures to live by, powers to tyrannize and to create beauty, induced joy and sorrow, in our efforts to spend our allotted times. Given nature's urge to live, these activities could be conducted with energy, and in an appropriate Aristotelian scenario have a beginning, a middle and an end. Only twice in the last few hundred years has the individual mind had cause to reflect on itself, to pause for reflection as it were.

The first was Newton's recognition of the heaviness of motion; the second was Einstein's recognition of the lightness of motion; but both were there from the beginning ... with mind. But neither were suitable to investigate with words, as Faraday's lines of force prompted him to ask Maxwell whether he could put his equations into words so that he (Faraday) might understand them. Gravity and light persisted as limits. Witness the great energy required to lift a capsule beyond the pull of gravity into space. Again, energy removed from a suitable element like uranium was devastating in its effect, as at Hiroshima, for the square of the speed of light, when combined with a mass, is an awesome matter.

Between these extremes lie Faraday's lines of force – present in the universe long before the cave drawings at Lascaux, but only given scientific precision in the nineteenth century. Maxwell's peculiar genius, however, greater even than Newton and Einstein, was to construct an abstract of the electromagnetic field and in a few equations provide, as the Greeks provided with the alphabet, simple components capable of enormous diversity. These simple equations of Maxwell are one of the glories of physics, inspiring the Austrian physicist Ludwig Boltzmann, his contemporary, to quote Goethe, 'Was it God who wrote these lines?'

The National had produced *The Wild Duck*. Ralph Richardson was playing Old Ekdal. During the run, David Storey had written a new play for him which he wanted to do so, so they asked me to take over. Considering the manifold fields that were slipping under my mind, I was extremely pleased to do. This was my first opportunity, since the moment in *Amadeus* when I'd reconciled myself to the grin of Mozart's equation, to observe Ibsen.

I had been interested in Brandes's efforts to link Kierkegaard and Ibsen, and Ibsen's crotchety response that he knew nothing of Kierkegaard, and that he'd read little of Kierkegaard and understood less. Given his technique of assembling his material over the eighteen months or so that a play was gestating, Ibsen's retorts are understandable, he was not an academic. He trusted his curiosity and brooding sufficiently to be able to recognize what chance might usefully put in his way. The merest particle might light up a movement in his equation.

Again, what was interesting was Brandes's reaction to *The Wild Duck*; it gave him little pleasure, and he never rated the play among Ibsen's greatest. It was clear that he did not detect anything in the play to inspire him to draw an analogy with a Copenhagen family.

The Wild Duck is about the interrelationship of two families, the Werle and Ekdal families. Ostensibly the dramatic interest is held on the stage by the actions of the Ekdal family. Yet the energy setting off these actions comes directly or indirectly from the Werle family. Once Ibsen had settled for prose his plays more and more hover round two people talking, until the movement reaches its fulfilment in *When We Dead Awaken*. *The Wild Duck* is the exception. The only way I can explain Ibsen's interest lies in the closeness between Denmark and Norway at the time. The scandal caused in Scandinavia by Kierkegaard's *Attack on Christendom* might have prompted Ibsen to that curiosity out of which many of his plays grow. At all events, I could now look closer at something I had suspected for a long time.

In his *Journals* Kierkegaard tells us:

> The dreadful case of a man who, when he was a little boy, suffered much hardship, was hungry, benumbed with cold, stood upon a hillock and cursed God – and the man was not able to forget this when he was eighty-two years old.

The boy was Michael Kierkegaard, Søren's father, who eventually came from Jutland to Copenhagen, and made a fortune as one of Copenhagen's leading drapers – which, to one of his nature, compounded his early sense of guilt. He was clearly a man of great energy for when his first wife died, within the year he had married Anne Lund, a peasant from Jutland, a servant in his house, who five months after the wedding presented him with the first son of their family. As one commentator puts it: 'The stern old man could never forgive himself for his incontinence.' It did not prevent him, however, from producing a family of seven, the youngest of whom was Søren Kierkegaard.

I was now using the field theory to relate the families, of Kierkegaard and Werle. I could not see the relationship, I could not see the field. Both anyway were abstract and unobservable. But if Ibsen, the dramatist, used the field theory, he might see some means of changing the Kierkegaard family into the time and space of the Werle family. So as an artist in the theatre can point our minds to the source of art, to life itself. Only there is the potential for new creation.

Some time before the play begins, old Werle and Old Ekdal had been in a kind of partnership, developing the forests of Norway. In some way (the unspecificity of many incidents surrounding the play is a source of strength), Old Werle had emerged as a tycoon, Old Ekdal as a failure. Both had sons. One eventually went to Germany at a time when the philosophy of Hegel was dominant; the other had to scratch a living as a photographer, with an illusion that he is an inventor.

The play opens with Gregers Werle, returning from Germany, at a dinner given by his father, with Hjalmar Ekdal, his old friend, as one of the guests. Through the party stumbles Old Ekdal, having come for some copy which the Werles hand out to him to keep him busy. Hjalmar wittingly fails to recognize his father.

The rest of the play takes place in the Ekdal household, a part of which has been converted into a domestic zoo for Old Ekdal's pets, one of whom, a wounded wild duck, causes special concern. Gina, many years earlier, had married Hjalmar. They have had one child, Hedvig. Gina had been a servant in the Werle household. Just before the play Old Ekdal marries Mrs Sörby, Werle's housekeeper. Like a true Hegelian, Gregers scents betrayal and begins to haunt the Werle household.

140

Old Werle is losing his sight. Hedvig's has always been weak. Gina, Hedvig's mother, once worked in the Ekdal household. Why does Old Ekdal receive work from Werle? Is there some blackmail to be uncovered? How old is Hedvig? When were Hjalmar and Gina married? Is Hjalmar sure that he is Hedvig's father? What is his invention, anyway? Faced with Gregers absolute for truth, Hjalmar has a furious row with Gina and, fuelled by his self-pity and weakness, leaves the house. Overwhelmed by the wretched condition to which Gregers has reduced her home, destroying her parents' happiness, Hedvig shoots herself in the attic, leaving the impression that she has shot the wounded wild duck. Temporarily, Gina and Hjalmar are reconciled by Hedvig's death. But there is little doubt that it is a shallow thing.

The tracery of the play, its resonances, its transformations, create an amazing field for the spectator to wonder at. Perhaps the most penetrating, Ibsen's transformation of Kierkegaard (as Gregers) into an Hegelian. This could only have been the result of an acute perception of the pressures of the times.

The years that I had been at the National had been enormously fruitful. Beginning with Bond's Greek play and ending with the Ibsen, they had affirmed the foundations of the theatre in my sense. My interest as an actor had always been to share the social and technical problems of the dramatist as they changed to give a momentary certainty in a continually moving world. Fashions could alter within decades, the sudden emergence of a great dramatist is unpredictable. But it had to do with the understanding of reality.

Milman Parry had given me the first clue in his suggestion that Homer's great epics are a sort of analogy of the society of their times. Maxwell had confirmed me in his mathematic analogy of the field to Faraday's lines of force. It was as though the Greeks had provided a range of foundation characters on which later dramatists were to improvise their innovations. Ibsen was to rock the foundation, and reach out to contemporary life. This was the impulse in *The Wild Duck* that made the play so important for all subsequent writers. To see in the Kierkegaard family, and especially in its genius of a son, an analogy for a pattern of dramatic movement was immediate insight. To mould and change that pattern according to his dramatic requirements was not only indicative of his great imaginative grasp, but was an astonishing example of how different fields of experience and growth interpenetrate society.

The analogy must not be stretched beyond its initial point of resemblance, otherwise it will become a copy. Was it this that attracted Joyce to Ibsen? *Ulysses* is the original insight and the wanderings of Odysseus in the Aegean, an analogy, but the novel as it evolves is uniquely Joyce and Dublin in a day.

I study politics a great deal as a movement of ideas between people that gradually assumes coherence in a political party or group. But I have never belonged to a political party, and I do not greatly admire those among my colleagues who feel they must express political opinions vociferously. They are very embarrassing. They have little idea how ugly they become, because they are so good at passion.

But I was forced to compare my situation in relation to the Edinburgh Fringe with that prevailing at the National Theatre. I felt that the openness of the Edinburgh venture with its occasional offence to taste harmonized much more than the National to a mood which I detected emerging in society, a move towards recognizing the autonomy of the individual. This was the other half of my feeling of revulsion for the crowd.

The problem in recognizing the autonomy of the individual lay in evolving a structure that, while providing a technique, yet left the autonomy intact – in this sense the Fringe Society was a model. But the model could only be maintained with a certain altruism. Towards the end of his Gifford Lectures, Sherrington introduces the notion of altruism as he measures the evolution of the nature of man through its movement towards the latest understanding of mind, which actually avoids him. But, without altruism, so dominant is man's mind over all the other species that they could be eliminated. Adam Smith called it sympathy. I called it interested detachment.

During the ten years I had been chairman of the Fringe Society I had practised a sort of altruism. I received no fee. I received my fares to Edinburgh. But when there I had paid all my own expenses. Only thus did I feel the concept of openness could be held intact, and provide an example of interested detachment that would be appropriate for the technique of all kinds of activity. I thought that Pericles of ancient Athens might have approved.

But the structure at the National was only the most immediate example of the kind of structure in our theatre that was preventing an open society. When I looked at the BBC and the IBA, the governing bodies that had inherited the fruits of Maxwell's differential equations, I found the conditions writ large that had discomfited me at the National. The nepotism, the repetition, the indignity of men as they sought for security and their own advancement, the acceptance of the competent instead of the expert, the ultimate laziness of thinking.

John Reith, the first Director-General of the BBC, was under the illusion, given the power of the new media of radio and television, that only the best, what he deemed of value, should be broadcast. He was in a powerful position to sustain his convictions since he presided over the richest heritage of literature and drama in the world. What he did not foresee was that Maxwell's discoveries initiated great new fields of diverse communication, and that repetition quickly induced boredom. The British Government, always philistine and fearful of the power of art, never truly analysed Maxwell's discoveries and how they might technically be applied to a society that was moving away from political parties towards individual autonomy.

The result was the setting up of organizations that were modelled on government departments. Reith's moral stance fitted the establishment's silent longing for justification. It had the received authority of the past. For the transmission of information the organizations were admirable and competent. They failed to recognize that the grounds of all art are radical and irrational.

As far as the organization and production of entertainment were concerned, the procedure established in the theatre was followed: the setting up of offices for reading scripts, organizing finance, casting and so on. What was disregarded was that Maxwell's fields could in a moment embrace the whole nation, tha novelty was exhausted in one display, that the whole library and museum of art that had been accumulated over three thousand years could be drained away in a few years of viewing. The result was an inward-looking, uncritical acceptance of their inadequacy by relying on a diminishing circle of experts who had been tried and could be relied on at least for repetition. Far from being open to innovation and diversity, radio and television became what is known in trade union circles as a 'closed shop'.

There were two areas in which the authorities were failing lamentably, in my view. Immediately after the war I gloried in the adventure of the Third Programme of the BBC. Starved of Europe, we were suddenly exposed to the richness of the continent's thought in science and the humanities. Over the years, as we have moved in on ourselves and become more insular, the radio adventure has become a mumble of superficial jargon, lacking depth and insight. I found this especially in the religious field. Instead of Reinhold Niebuhr, Bultmann and Bonhoeffer we have been subjected to the enthusiasms of minor Christian sects, and a surrender to trite fundamentalist theology from the United States. It is impossible to take any religious broadcast seriously.

Again, this has been accompanied by a disgraceful lapse in standards of diction. There is scarcely a voice without blemishes. Few can inflect correctly. It is a great temptation because of its apparent simplicity to take English for granted.

I was really being very silly and pompous in leaving the National. It was not a question whether anyone would listen to me. It was a question whether I would listen to myself. I was playing things the wrong way round. In terms of ancient Greek drama, this was the satyr after the show, without the show. What was the show? What was intriguing me at this time?

Since Hiroshima, peace has been established in Europe. With peace the structures of power in politics and religion have slowly been eroded, chiefly because the principles on which any politics or religion is founded have been declared obsolete by the fundamental truth of science that everything moves, the world is never at rest. It is a situation in which an artist may feel he has an entitlement to say something. Nothing of great importance, nothing like a manifesto. But someone who is at one remove from being an artist, someone like an actor, because he acts individuals might have something to say about the individual. Now that politics and religion have over a long time failed us, the individual may even wish to be an actor and create himself.

Repetition is like a drug in the theatre, and I now appreciated the motive of actors who wanted to limit their time in successful plays, particularly in view of the vulnerability of my colleagues at the National, some of whom could hardly dare to submit themselves to the blast of the commercial world. I was old enough to see a stalemate all around me. Where to turn?

16 The Price

It was now 1982, and I was 74. Some company had presented Shaw's *Getting Married* very successfully at the Yvonne Arnaud Theatre in Guildford, and it was decided a little later to open the Malvern Festival with the play. Richard Vernon, who had played the Bishop, was unable to do so and I was asked to take up the part, being warned that I would only have a fortnight's rehearsal at the most. The prospect of playing in Shaw at Malvern was irresistible. Curigwen had played Dolly in *You Never Can Tell* during one of the festivals before the war, and of course Jane Eyre before coming to London. Besides, for a Scotsman, the flow of the land from Shropshire and the Malvern Hills down the Thames to Oxford and London has a special grace.

The cast was excellent; the director, Clifford Williams; rehearsals, a delight. The play opened well without a hitch. The second night, too, began hopefully, and the first act played beautifully. Then half-way through the second act, in a scene with Barbara Leigh-Hunt, I dried. For a moment of stillness that seemed like hours, I peered at the play and myself. The clutter of preoccupations that had concerned me over the years burst in from my fantastic imagination without hindrance, and became confused with Shaw's lines. They lay before my mind as on a field. But I could not find the will to go on. I had lost the power to choose. My position was static – movement was denied to me. My mind was stunned by the speed of it all. Then, from my imagination, emerged a story I had been told about Ralph Richardson. Playing *Macbeth* at Stratford in the mid-fifties, he had dried, and quite nonchalantly walked over to the prompt corner, took up the prompt copy, and carried it on to the stage, reading the part as though nothing had happened.

I found myself reading from the prompt copy, and following the stage directions I took my place on a seat next to Barbara, at which point my sight became a trifle blurred. Ian Lavender, who was standing in the wings, noticed my difficulty, went to my dressing-room and returned with my spectacles, which I gravely took from him, and then I went on reading the part. All this time I had heard no sound from the audience except the occasional titter at Shaw's lines. The scene ended, and I left the stage. There was a curious silence. My colleagues nodded to me. Shortly I entered for the last scene by which time I had recovered and returned the prompt copy to its corner. We took our curtains. The audience applauded. Everyone seemed to be moving slowly, as on the floor of a swimming pool.

Astonishingly, I felt well. John Harcop, the theatre doctor, who examined me immediately after the play, said my blood pressure was what might be expected, a trifle high but not catastrophically so. I was very still. The usual dry is short, and recovery is hardly noticeable. This dry of mine was dramatic, massive, and in a way final. My colleagues did not seem to see it as anything more than a temporary lapse of concentration; I heard one murmur it was sad. But generally their response was mature and professional – total silence. Though they would for the next few days drop in at my hotel, and ask if I was all right.

Of course I was all right. I could have told them I had made an enormous discovery, and that my dry was the painful occasion of it. I hadn't quite thought it out. But I could, of course – I had my memory. The actor's imagination is primary, intuitive, spontaneous and immediate. I had unwittingly allowed my own personal imagination to visit it. I had been caught in the swing doors. I had not learned then how to use Maxwell's demon, the controlling guardian between the cells in my field equation. I smiled because I could put it differently.

The long moment of my dry was a period of incognito – I was neither myself or the part. But I was clearly occupying some field. For a long moment I had no identity. It was as though my imagination and my memory were fighting to take possession of my mind. My imagination was pelting my mind with particles of ideas moving at devastating speed while my memory was telling me to take it easy. There was really no need to be in such a hurry. Eventually, my imagination got tired or bored with the fight and went to sleep, leaving my memory in possession of my mind and my part. It was just common sense, I told myself, while the doctor took my blood pressure.

He drove me to my hotel. On the journey I felt something of Raskolnikov's temptation to hover round his actions by telling John Harcop of my surprise at what I had done because ever since the war I had been preoccupied by the actor's memory, and what it could tell us about the nature of mind. 'All matter, all life,' says Sherrington 'is granular – but not mind.' And Erwin Schrödinger, the pioneer of wave mechanics, agrees that the mind is still inaccessible to the physiologist. It turned out that John was a bit of a psychiatrist. I told him that the solution to the nature of mind did not lie through the treatment of illness, but must involve, so I thought, new concepts of imagination and movement, of time and space. He said goodnight, and told me to write a book.

For a long time now I've not taken supper after playing. A glass of whisky and water is enough to still my feelings. This time I took a large whisky and milk to my room, and phoned Curigwen to tell her what I'd done.

'Are you well?' she asked.

I said, 'Yes, terribly well.'

'Good,' she said, 'that's all right then. It's not the end of the world.'

She was coming down to Malvern later. Yes, I was well. I might have collapsed. I might have had a nervous breakdown. Had I as the Bishop experienced what people called schizophrenia? That boggled my imagination.

After talking to Curigwen, I sat at my window looking out over the Malvern Hills, that fall of the cello line in the Elgar concerto getting mixed up with the Count's in the last act of *Figaro*, and the horn tune in Richard Strauss's *Don Juan*. The speed with which things associated themselves in the mind! Then I shuddered. For a moment I was overwhelmed with the enormity of what I had done. I had offended that great line of actors that stretches from Sophocles down through Shakespeare to Noel Coward. It made me giggle as I recalled that Greek actor in the theatre of Dionysus who, weighed down with the paraphernalia of the classical actor fell over sideways. They had to bring a crane to lift him up. And Lewis Casson in Gielgud's *Lear*! Sometimes Lewis would dry. Then he would stamp his feet, turn his back on the audience, thread his way upstage, mumbling, 'De-da-de-da de-da/Da-de. da-de da-de/da until he remembered his passage. It was easy to do that with Shakespeare's verse; not so easy with Shaw's prose. I was alternating my sense of guilt with excuses.

As I settled down in my bed two thoughts occurred to me. For the second time I had disproved the Cartesian duality, that man is composed of mind and body. He had omitted what unites the two, the imagination. The second thought was a saying of Yeats, that a man is nothing until related to an image. I was in a mood to subscribe to that.

147

But what image? That I had desperately to seek.

I woke the next day, knowing that my task would not be easy. Fortunately I had two days before the next performance of the play, which gave me a little time to adjust to the situation. I was seventy-four, and though aware that nine days' rehearsal were too few for me to acquire the groove of the part, nevertheless realized this was an aspect of the new materialistic theatre I had to accept. I recalled for a moment with nostalgia the long rehearsal periods at the National.

My dry had proved that I could recover in a flash all the things on which my imagination had been brooding. The immediate problem was to find some image to control them, so that my actor's mind and memory would not be subjected to some volatile disruption by them. I was in a strange way aware that I was dealing with abstract entities as though they were real and physical. Clearly the part must be the centre of any programme. Though I knew it, I decided to repeat it twice a day, after breakfast and lunch. Although I did not appear until twenty minutes after curtain up, I would be in the theatre an hour before for the wardrobe mistress to dress me. I then followed my usual technique. I would sit quietly while I went through the movements I made in the play, making a geometrical pattern in my mind. I can now relax so that after a brief period I feel that a wind has blown through my mind, and the molecules of my body are not at cross-purposes.

But what of this image? What sort of image did Yeats have in mind? There was a line in the play that I had as the Bishop that stuck with me. Speaking of marriage he says, 'Until the laws of marriage are first made human, they can never become divine.' Up to now everything descended on us from above, including our ideas about the mind. If we could find something common to all minds, then we might be in a way to respect the individual mind, as we were beginning to respect the gene, after Crick and Watson.

Meanwhile, by an act of will, sometimes tiring, I was able to concentrate my memory on the part. There were still nervous tics though and it required a high degree of concentration to get through the first week at Malvern. I was acutely aware that I was in the situation, 'Actor! Heal thyself.'

Curigwen came down during the second week and caught a performance. She noticed nothing untoward. And business was very good. Shaw had called her the girl with the unpronounceable name. When she had played Dolly in *You Never Can Tell*, he had given her a line, not in the script that he'd given to Dorothy Minto. His mind always leapfrogged back to the first production of his plays. It was altogether very moving for her. Jane Eyre still has a special place for her.

After Malvern we took the play to Richmond, so I was able to live at home. The weather was wonderful. Too like London in 1939 and 1940 not to stir an uneasiness. I was deeply aware of a change in the moral climate. We were in the middle of the Falklands adventure. Then to Cardiff, where my will continued to unite the mind and its nervous body in harmony. And we were doing superb business, but then Shaw, especially in comedy, always does well. Next was York, to be reached through London; it is now only two hours by train from London. I decided to stay at home until the Monday.

I was very familiar with the train journey to York and beyond, as every month or so I travelled up to Edinburgh for meetings of the Edinburgh Festival Fringe Society. Travelling up the east coast of Britain, which I love, it's easy to transport yourself into the Middle Ages as you pass in succession, mostly on your right, the tired, gracious monuments of the Church at Peterborough, Selby, York, Durham and Newcastle, the knots of the Catholic Province round which hover the particles of the parish churches which the Benedictines have scattered.

Passing Peterborough, I suddenly decided to use York to review how I now stood. It was an idea which caught on and by the time I reached York my spirit was renewed, and I became excited. My rooms were in a boarding house just off the road to York Minster, a nice walk of twenty minutes which I decided to take every morning. To the theatre that night, where the play opened to a packed house, and was received jovially. I was now completely at ease. I could participate in the hospitality after the show without embarrassment. And back to my rooms and tomorrow.

15 June 1982. For me I was out quite early, just before ten. The weather smiled. York is, apart from anything else, a holiday town, so I had to thread my way through crowds of visitors on my way to the Minster. Inside, the building sighed with the low hum of distant bees as lines of oddly assorted visitors, whispering in tongues, wound slowly round the aisles, pausing just long enough at the recumbent tombs, to be puzzled by them.

The Minster is immense, with the great east window shedding a saffron pallor over the interior of the building; a great overcoat protected the unvarnished cross. The cathedral sprouted a vast assortment of ideas which, as usual, atom-like, pierced my mind. I sat down at the end of a pew, looking towards the altar. Where to begin? I was acutely aware of being between two worlds. The world of physical reality, everyday living, and the abstract world. This was not what we normally think of as abstract. This was abstract because it could not be seen or measured, but it was real enough. The mind, Hiroshima, radio and television proved its existence. I must begin with time. This was where the Greeks had begun. Chronology triumphant! Chronos married the Earth, and begat Zeus, the father of the gods. God, according to another source, made the earth and all that is in it in seven days. Seven days! Here, too, in this vast space, time spelt out its measure of passage, but now there was only the timid quartering of the hour.

In the Middle Ages, a variety of measures marked the passage. Bells, bells, all the time, of one kind or another, a harmony of noise. Then, the church offices of the day as God ordained its reckoning from prime, at the rising of the sun, to compline, at its fading. Monks in their stalls, reading the dialectic of psalms as the mood of the day grew in brightness until it was hushed in the darkness of night. Then, too, punctured throughout the day with random decision, the processions of great dignitaries of the Church, surrounded by their trains of acolytes, bell-ringers, trumpeters, sackbut players moaning and groaning, and bells again, noise announcing presence and status within an earthly hierarchy pretending to copy heaven.

Now, all I could see was a scruffy clergyman fidgeting his way through the crowd to a side-chapel to conduct morning prayers.

What did it all betoken, this decline of the great Church to a whimper of reverence? As I sat in my pew, two things. A great revulsion to repetition. A repetition that belonged to the heaviness of things, and bore no relation to the new world of light, of fluxions, and vortices, volatility and danger, the light of new creation, of openness and surprise. Again, this repetition of mumbo-jumbo denied the individual. It assumed a place for all according to divine prediction. At least, so it was interpreted. Hierarchy rejected freedom. It had to, in order to maintain its structure. Shaw was right, people had to become human, before they could become divine. My first day in the Minster had, I thought, been fruitful, pinpointing two of the threads surrounding my mind. I joined the crowd as they departed for lunch.

16 June. Last night was a repeat of the first night. About repetition I must be very careful since acting and the theatre involved repetition.

Today, before going into the Minster I walked on the Roman Wall. This, too, had lasted, if a little worn at the edges. In their time men live the illusion that the symbols and artefacts of their insights will be permanent. The insights move on, the symbols and artefacts remain as tombstones? No, not quite so. Here was a wall existing long after its Empire had collapsed, there a Minster lingering on in hope. I was not the artist who condemned them to the museum. The artist insisted that we must see all things new. Even ruins hold some truth that will make us richer. I had done for the moment with the artefacts. What of the symbols? I went into the Minster. This time I moved closer to the altar. However interesting I found the details of the ambience, my eyes always came back to the cross. However rich the surrounding decorations, they paled into insignificance compared to the buoyancy of this simple cross. Eventually I was so bemused by its appeal that I had to will myself to look away from it. But as I did, the thought crossed my mind that this was all that was left of Christianity. Everything else was only approximation. The apostles, the saints, the resurrection of the body, the life everlasting. What did they mean in the now of experience, of lovers facing each other in their sensuality, the now of failure, the now of the self in its self-awareness. I turned towards the cross. Indeed did I know myself without this cross? I thought of William of Occam, the medieval philosopher. He was the first thinker to emphasize the difference between a thinker reflecting, and an individual existing. What was I doing, reflecting or existing?

I thought gratefully of Yeats. I had found my image; and the strange thing was it had ceased to be just a symbol. It had become a reality that could live in my mind, asserting itself, so I thought, of its own accord. I thought of Maxwell and his demons. But this was not a demon. It was my will, guarding the doors between my mind, memory and imagination. Directing those things which enriched my openness to others, and controlling those feelings that diminished me. Indeed, I felt a human being, if I could ever know what that was. But my ignorance was a necessity. Had I known what the individual was, I would have joined one of those parties or religions that have inside information and are so anxious to spread it. This way I knew I was free. No reflecting. Existing, existing now. It had taken a long time. And there was more to do. The Minster had served its turn; I did not come to it again.

What had happened at York, of course, was the coming together consciously of what had been coming together for a long time. Indeed, any time over the last twenty years I might have picked out a moment when my will and a symbol came together to make up an image. What gave it significance now was my recovery from the dry. For the performances at the Theatre Royal continued to draw full and responsive houses. My colleagues were even murmuring about the play going to the West End after the tour, which had some dates to finish.

What was the difference between an image and a symbol? What did

Yeats mean by an image? Why did I find a heightened awareness of myself when I brought together two simple things, my will and a cross? What changed the symbol into a permanent image? Were Ibsen's symbols images? A symbol is the sign that recognizes the link between two objects and possesses the potential of movement. But that was my own definition in the twentieth century. It was not so in the Middle Ages. Then, symbolist thought permitted an infinity of relations between things, and each thing might denote a number of distinct ideas by its different special qualities. The highest conceptions had symbols by the thousand. Nothing is too humble to represent and glorify the sublime. For instance, the Dutch historian J. Huizinga points out, 'The walnut signifies Christ; the sweet kernel is his divine nature, the green and pulpy outer peel is His humanity, the wooden shell between is the cross. Thus all things raise the thoughts to the eternal, being thought of as symbols of the highest, in a constant gradation, they are all transfused by the glory of divine majesty. Every precious stone sparkles with the brilliance of its symbolic value.' There is a moment in Ibsen's last play when the sculptor is self-indulgently weeping crocodile tears over the deceptions he has practised in his art. Irene looks at him contemptuously, then hisses, 'Poet!'

There is no greater difference between the objectivity of the pre-Copernican world, with its profusion of symbols, and the subjectivity of the Einstein world than in the use of language. The classical world seeks wholeness through the descent of knowledge; the modern world creates wholeness through acknowledging difference. One night the actor is involved in describing the voluptuous differences that make up Cleopatra's barge; the next in wrestling with the stark monosyllables of solitude in Beckett.

I felt that art and science were coming together in the modern world. They needed each other in a way that was not necessary in the classical framework. This had to do, in some way, with energy. The energy that the medieval thinker found in the walnut to trace Christ's attributes relative to its parts is not available now. Had not Herbert Butterfield, after examining Christianity in European history, concluded that the only guidance it could give in our time was to hold fast to Christ, and for the rest go uncommitted?

There was a ground of insight that was present in both art and science. Was there not a coherence between Ibsen's recognition that, while he could start with Kierkegaard, the progress thereafter must be his own, and Maxwell's insight that Faraday's lines of force needed his own unique mathematics to transform them into universal fields. There were two great insights in Einstein's equation that embraced both Ibsen and Maxwell.

The revolutionary element in Einstein's theory is not only that it is true in matters of energy, mass and time which can be scientifically proved as it was at Hiroshima. It is true also in human affairs. But then only as it applies to the individual. It cannot apply to any kind of collective. It is not entirely irrelevant that the first question that occurred to Einstein's scientific mind was, 'What would the world look like if I was sitting on a beam of light?' We are all sitting on our own beams of light now.

York provided no more problems. The play completed the week, doing good business; and I was myself again. I had expected my journey from York to Nottingham on a Sunday to be something of a tussle through crowds of young people escaping in search of pleasure. But no. The stations were empty, such benches on the platform as were occupied held a sprinkling of the old and very young with a clutch of bulging plastic bags round their feet. I had a carriage to myself.

I changed trains at Sheffield. There was the quiet of Sunday all about me. I could see here what I had recognized so frequently on my journeys to Scotland. The great care put into the countryside, the husbandry was so excellent in its measure of time and space and design. And we were at war.

In Nottingham I was booked in at the Strathdon Hotel, close to the theatre. The Don is one of those rivers (the other is the Dee), that embrace Aberdeen on their way to the sea. Hotel groups, like Plato, begin with the naming of things. The hotel group is called the Thistle. There is occasionally a breathtaking obviousness about things. The Strathdon is one of those hotels built since the war for travellers expected to pass through quickly. The bedrooms are like monks' cells in size, essentially furnished with a Gideon Bible tucked away at the side of the bed. It was similar to the Abbey Motor Hotel in Leicester where I had struggled with *When We Dead Awaken*.

The difference between Suez and the Falklands was one of light. The arguments, reasons, justifications surrounding Suez in 1956 were opaque and ambiguous; the reason for the Falklands was as clear as day; at least so I thought. We had endured Vietnam, and in Cambodia realized with horror that genocide in spite of the Holocaust still existed. The Russians had invaded Afghanistan. All wars of a kind, but none large enough to embroil the world. And then the Falklands! Whatever arguments were advanced about sovereignty, or the historic situation through which these islands became British and were occupied by people who had chosen to be British, to my mind the Argentine invasion to change the status quo was uncivilized, and could never be justified. By democratic procedure, by suffrage, by enlightened argument, yes, but by war, no.

Initially then, I was much clearer about the Falklands than I ever felt about Suez. And yet the situation of war, like one of Maxwell's fields, in the twentieth century had been given a new equation. The differential had been provided by Hiroshima. The example of Hiroshima and then Nagasaki, the one repetition in all history to justify its message, was so profound that the final solution could not be contemplated, even by mistake. Short of that, then, local wars had to be accepted, even if only to raise nations to that level of suffering that induces true pain and humility. Indeed, I now saw suffering as the universal experience for all individuals, as they created paradoxically their style of life and grace of living.

Nottingham confirmed York; the audiences were ample and enthusiastic. I was now so relaxed that I could rejoice in the careless lightness with which the company was playing Shaw.

I find that when I'm involved in a problem my mind, memory and imagination tighten up like a spring, to be released with the solution. But this time, only halfway. It was absurd, really, that I would ever be able to tell myself that I had solved the problem of the nuclear bomb. Yet it is a matter for individual decision, and the symbol of Hiroshima would lie alongside the cross, as one of the guardians of my mind.

But why was I uneasy? J. Bronowski says the magical number is two; faced with the quantum physicist Werner Heisenberg's problem of uncertainty, Niels Bohr looked up at him and murmured, 'Complementarity!' Hiroshima was the devastating echo when men released nature. What kind of echo of his nature did man release? We had to walk dangerously between Scylla and Charybdis. I had embraced my Scylla. Where could I find Charybdis? I had already found it in Cambodia, in Pol Pot. But he had a model.

In the spring of 1942 (I was in the army then), Hitler had held a conference of his High Command in Berlin. He ordered the extermination of the Jewish race. I could only see individuals. He ordered six factories to be built in Poland for the purpose. I called them extermination factories. Treblinka was the name I seized on. Here was my complementarity. Man emulating nature in exterminating his own. This was the Scylla and Charybdis of our century, Hiroshima and Treblinka; my cross had two lengths. The magical number was indeed two.

The tour continued running into the sands of repetition, the play had thrown a great light on myself.

154

For some time now Curigwen and I had been alone. The family had grown up and departed. Indeed Harriet had married and, like her mother, produced three children, two girls and a boy. Marty and Johnny were very independent. None of them was a Christian, in the sense of belonging to a Church.

In August there was the Edinburgh Festival. The size of the Fringe was increasing enormously, as it was bound to, given the economic conditions existing in the West. A new Conservative government had been elected in 1979. and was feeling its way in the right direction without really knowing why. There was no Hume or Adam Smith to tell them. It was part of the educational assumption in England, that had not existed in Scotland, that specialism and separation in subjects should be encouraged. The notion that an actor might have ideas about science, religion, or economics was absurd. It was absurd to me, too, but I had them. I couldn't help it. My education had spread over all the fields.

But there was a more profound reason. Complementary to Kierkegaard's category of the individual, there had grown up in Europe what is called an existential relation between things, which is really no more than seeing people and things interrelated in one world, yet having their own individual identity and authenticity. Of people in freedom, growing in self-awareness and through relationship learning the truth about themselves. It was a pity that most English thinkers found the word 'existential' pompous and superior. It had much of Occam in it. On the continent, it was absorbed naturally and indirectly into a general mode of thinking. Fundamentally, this was a move towards the individual and adapting social organizations so that they would increase freedom, the ground of individual choice.

The speed with which the new views were being practised in France and Germany would have shattered all political and religious thought but for the fact that, to follow Occam again, existence is to be lived, something different from reflection.

It was now 1983, and following on the temporarily successful outcome of the Falklands affair, the government was swept back into power through its popularity, covertly suggesting in its manifesto that it would proceed with its policy of selling council houses, and what was erroneously called the 'privatization' of public assets. What the Conservatives had done in their two administrations since 1979 were the first steps in recognizing the primacy of the individual in society. In this, it was proving a model. Not because there was any great thinker in the Conservative Party, but because the situation of Britain, its existential measure in time and space, was directing the government to

155

solve their problems this way, in contrast to the collective solutions sought in a Communist-dominated economy. In every field of life, there was tension between the individual and the collective enterprise.

'Look to your maps' is a maxim that all thinkers must bear in mind. I think that all my life I have been acutely aware of the flow of ideas as men pursue them over land and water, their dying and rebirth. One of the reasons that lay behind my acceptance of the chairmanship of the Fringe Society was that Scotland lay on the margin of Europe, an open space that allowed Europeans to breathe and express themselves in art of their own choosing.

My view of Britain has always been as part of Europe. The Empire grew at a time when small armies could triumph in large places. The growth occurred at a time (in the main, the eighteenth century) when the great flurry of scientific discovery in the seventeenth century led on to the industrialization of the eighteenth century, with one addition; Adam Smith's *The Wealth of Nations* provided the financial technique to hold the vastly different enterprises together. We forget that, with Hume, Adam Smith was regarded as one of the pillars of the major eighteenth-century philosophical movement, the Enlightenment. Lastly, Britain itself as a country was compact, and held the exit door from Europe to America and the rest of the world.

In the twentieth century, it is the compactness of Britain that makes it a prime area for the experiment of solving the problems of a volatile world of great complexity. One prophecy of Marx's that was profoundly wrong suggesting that he did not really understand what he was about, was that Communism would arrive firstly in an industrial society. And for one very simple reason: he did not understand that the world was moving towards light and the individual. Newton had made sure of that.

I was now seventy-five. The individual and light, freedom and choice, the untruth of the crowd, were becoming obsessions with me which caused me a great deal of jollity. I was also so delighted with my discovery of Maxwell's fields that I felt sure, such was the confidence I had in the West's scientific expertness, the few channels of television we were limited to by an unimaginative government would expand enormously. I wanted them to. It was the only practical way I could see of fulfilling my dictum, 'We are all artists now'. Just as over the years I had seen young people on the Fringe presenting their problems of identity indirectly through Eliot, Lawrence, Joyce, the Czech Franz Kafka, the American Emily Dickinson, yes and the Russians Anna Akhmatova and Osip and Nadezhda Mandelstam, so the time would come when they themselves would reveal the layers of feelings and hates that composed their inwardness.

156

In 1983 I warned my colleagues on the Fringe that I wanted to resign. In 1984 I did it. One night, when we were watching the six o'clock news, the telephone rang. Curigwen, who is older than me but much more agile, answered it. 'It's Tom Fleming,' she said on her return, 'He's ringing from Glasgow.' I listened to Tom. For a moment I couldn't believe it. The Scottish Theatre Company were going to do Lindsay's *The Thrie Estaites* at the Edinburgh Festival. Would I be free? And what part would I like to play? He mentioned two parts. I said the smallest. A lecherous Abbot? Certainly, I said that a lecherous Abbot would suit me nicely. At the National I had repeated myself with a difference, now again I was going to repeat myself with a partial difference, this time I would complete the equation. Or so I thought.

17 Memories

The idea of doing *The Thrie Estaites* revived memories of Tyrone Guthrie and the modern *Hamlet* of 1938; and, now that I was getting on, particularly the older men in that cast. Two had stood out. O. B. Clarence, an actor from the turn of the century, played Polonius with a light detachment in his neat, careful moves. He really painted his make-up on with brushes, in the process taking years off his age. Old actors tend to grow younger.

Not so with Craighall Sherry. He was a discovery and rehabilitation of Guthrie's. He was an old Scots actor of the vintage of Hay Petrie, Matheson Lang and the young Will Fyffe. Much of his life had been spent in early films. Now old but still erect, his mind was retreating almost visibly. It was easy to see why Guthrie had cast him for the Player King. His face seemed to be moulded from horn, a startling white flecked with brown, thick sensuous lips, a bald head, and two staring eyes held in a constant intentness gazing elsewhere. His voice was thick but clear; like me, he gave true value to words like 'hugger-mugger' that sprouted their meaning. Meg Christie, from Canada, looked after him, guiding him on to the stage, and giving him his cues. Otherwise, he sat by the stage, passive and erect.

Why do such actors hold such life in their bodies? Were they in some mystical sense the receptacles of particles of pain that had been in orbit since fifth-century Athens? If they burst into speech would they, like the foot-infected Greek bowman Philoctetes, splutter their hatred on society? Now that I was leaving the Fringe, I was brooding on a one-man show involving the dummies of the prophet Ecclesiastes, Philoctetes and Sartre, expressing through them feelings of hate, much

158

on the line of Sartre's 'I must hate you because I know no other way of loving you!' Our theatre was becoming too docile. This momentary feeling of mine was due to my exasperation at the lack of openness in our society. Particularly as I saw it in the theatre and television. If ideas do not expand, they contract. We were in a contracting, reducing phase. Beating time before waiting to take off.

The Thrie Estaites was a great success, due, I think, to the colour and energy of the production. It suited the Assembly Hall admirably, so much so the company was invited to repeat the production the following year. Before I rejoined the company for that, I fitted in a play of Rodney Ackland's – *Smithereens*, at the Theatre Royal, Windsor. The producer was Lee Menzies, who told me that he was doing a play later on in which there was a part of a judge he would like me to play.

Ackland, with Ronald Mackenzie, had been one of the bright hopes of the theatre between the wars. His play was literate, civilized, one of which I should have approved, yet something was missing. I concluded it was myself. What was it? Why was it happening now? Not ten years ago, I had found acting in the last Ibsen exciting and satisfying. There was a great bleating about entertainment. Racine called his plays entertainments! Plenty of violence on television, little in the theatre. It was going against the grain to be so reasonable. The great dramatists had thrived on the irrational. In the meantime, the theatre would explore the minor masterpieces of Europe. From Spain, Vienna, the fringe dramatists of Elizabethan England, revivals, and musicals attempting to prove that our culture was moving in a new direction. There was so much that it was difficult to detect the novel and exciting. We were only beginning to glimpse the problems and possibilities that Maxwell's waves were providing for communication.

In the autumn of 1986, I was suddenly hailed by the Scottish Theatre Company to repeat *The Thrie Estaites*. The company had been invited to take part in the Warsaw Theatre Festival. With the help of some Glasgow businessmen, they had scrambled enough money together to get the company to Warsaw. The project was to last just a week. Three performances in Glasgow, fly to Warsaw, three performances there, then return home immediately.

We flew from Prestwick on a bleak November day in an ancient Polish army plane that just managed to lift itself off the ground, then hedgehopped its way to Warsaw at a modest cruising speed. I was sitting near the front and for four hours had the animated fractious hum of the propellers about my head. A year or so earlier, I had spent a weekend in Budapest on a lengthy film venture Tony Palmer was

159

concocting about Wagner, and I was not surprised to meet a similar atmosphere in Warsaw. It is not just that the colours have a uniform lack of interest, but all movement seems deprived of purpose.

We were all staying in a large hotel, the Forum, built by Americans, in a now-universal style of tourist equipment. The theatre was different, and retained some aspects of traditional continental theatre. The attendants at the dressing rooms were middle-aged women, soberly dressed, with little aprons to signify their function. The Poles were charming, in spite of the impossibility of finding any subject to talk to them about. Some nodded when I mentioned Kierkegaard. They were from Cracow University, aware perhaps of their Copernican tradition. Yet I had only to see a line of poplars shivering in the light mist, and my mind was transported to the nineteenth century; to Pushkin and his great verse-novel *Eugene Onegin*, and the real beginning of Russian literature. Another space in the cosmos of my mind, the space from Leningrad to Warsaw, and that burst of literature and music that embraces Dostoevsky and Shostakovich.

Home again, and a similar experience in the reverse direction, to be greeted at Prestwick with a fight for the buses to take us back to Glasgow. It had all been accomplished within the week, and I was very tired.

Two days later, watching television with Curigwen, I collapsed. At least I assumed I had, because I woke up in a small room in Westminster Hospital, lying on an operating table, surrounded by the family peering down at me.

After a long silence, they explained what had happened. Perhaps it was because of my recent moves that the first thought that occurred to me was the astronaut Yuri Gagarin's. Orbiting the earth for the first time in 1961, he announced, 'There is no God.' Emerging from the deep impenetrability of my black void, I found more comfort in Einstein's 'Subtle is the Lord; malicious he is not.'

I stayed in Westminster Hospital for four days. The doctors could find nothing wrong with me, but they gave me a thorough examination for which I was grateful. I would not have had one otherwise.

18 Beyond Reasonable Doubt

Some months into the new year of 1987 I received the manuscript of *Beyond Reasonable Doubt*, a play by politician-turned-writer Jeffrey Archer. This was the play that Lee Menzies had mentioned to me the year previously at Windsor. In the meantime there had developed over the whole enterprise something of a foggy blur in that Archer had become involved with a national newspaper over some libellous matter. The play had received a bouquet. Ambiguity had been conferred on it. For if Archer lost his case, there would be some sympathy for him. However, if the verdict went otherwise and the newspaper lost, the atmosphere surrounding the play, and its reception by the press, would be unpredictable, verging from the prickly to the paranoiac. Such was Archer's political, business and literary history and the complex reactions to it in the newspaper world, the play would not be seen, as it were, clear.

In being interviewed about the play, I always made the point of the similarity I found between Archer and Sir Walter Scott. In the first decades of the nineteenth century, Scott, with *The Lay of the Last Minstrel* (1808) and *Marmion* (1810), had established himself as perhaps the leading poet in Britain. Caught up with the financially inefficient Edinburgh publishing houses of Ballantyne and Constable, Scott found himself in 1826 in the deep embarrassment of being on the verge of bankruptcy. Having already with great energy turned from poetry to prose, from verse to romance for which he always hankered, and published some twenty of the Waverley novels anonymously, he wrote his way out of debt in half a dozen years, possibly shortening his life in the process, but acknowledging his authorship in 1827.

161

Somewhat similarly, Archer, when an MP, had found himself in a position akin to Scott's and with a like energy turned to the telling of stories to retrieve his fortunes, though not anonymously. Both novelists were richly rewarded. Unlike Archer, Scott had a nose for bankruptcy, almost seeking it out; Archer turned to the theatre.

With the court case looming, I read the play with great care.

When reading a manuscript for the first time, I think most actors are like me – they give the play the benefit of the doubt. As their livelihood is involved, they must see the best in the play so that their playing will be grounded in confidence. I have never understood actors who are cynical about their work; sceptical, yes, but cynical, no. It was my scepticism about the virtue of Ibsen's characters that provided much of the stimulus in acting them.

The play was a simple story. It was the form that was surprising. The first act is occupied by a court scene; the trial of Metcalfe, a leading figure of the law, the Chairman of the Bar Council, for the murder of his wife. He conducts his own case. The trial evokes the circumstances of their lives, the suffering of his wife from cancer, and their enduring differences of opinion about the poetry of Dylan Thomas and cricket.

The first four scenes of the second act lead up to the death of his wife; the last scene, to the eventual confession of the husband and his suicide.

In view of my preoccupations with Einstein and Maxwell at this time, what firstly attracted me was the experiment with time. This was quite unlike any of J. B. Priestley's dramatic experiments, where (despite some odd loops) time was still seen as a linear progression from past to future. In this play, time is seen as a vertical structure in that events are recorded in a pseudo-final situation through a trial, and then replayed as they originally occurred. The audience is in the position to compare the similarities and disparities of the two versions, and decide on a verdict. I was sick of conventional plotting, and thought that one way in which our theatre could be rescued from boring repetition was to see action leaping into the present moment of time.

Science, unlike art, abolishes history. The emotions, relationships, comedies and tragedies of humanity were established early and have a wonderful zest in repeating themselves. They are impervious to time.

This was Sherrington's problem. He could not understand how science had come to know so much, so quickly, about material reality, but so little about the mind and personality. Science explored the environment in time, and as our view of time changed, so a new frame was provided for art. As at this time, the 'now' of the present moment, the now of the mind. I felt this play was moving in that direction.

My second reason for embracing the play was the human element.

One problem for our instant, sensual society is incompatibility. The immediate recognition through sex of complementary pleasure clearly encourages many young people to embark on marriage without any real knowledge of the layers of sensibility that make up individuals, and they are unable to cope when differences appear.

I saw the Metcalfes' use of their differences over Dylan Thomas and cricket as a modest exercise in coping with incompatibility. For these reasons I was persuaded by the play, and I still am.

As the weeks passed, it emerged quite arbitrarily that the court case and the rehearsal period would collide. On the periphery of this central activity, the theatres we were to play at were opened for booking and practically closed on the same day. Jeffrey Archer's activities were of absorbing interest to the public. It was not only his career but the massive energy he displayed in his work that made him a source of endless public curiosity. What is more, he had achievements that could be measured. The more I saw of him, the more closely he resembled Scott.

Before the case and rehearsals started, he invited the cast to meet him in his flat overlooking the Houses of Parliament and with a view of the Thames towards Tower Bridge. As the lights came up along the Embankment, the scene settled down to an early evening doze, the cast mumbling their pleasure at meeting old friends and appraising new ones. Mary Archer, his wife, was a surprise. She might have been Jeffrey's sister, same height and colouring. I gossiped about the past. I said nothing about the case.

Rehearsals started on 20 July at Petyt House, by the church at the foot of Old Church Street. I realized suddenly that I was in very familiar territory. In 1933, after the tour of E. M. Delafield's *To See Ourselves*, my first wife, Stella, and I had set up in a flat not fifty yards from the rehearsal room. Later on, I had bought a short lease on a small house in Glebe Place, just round the corner from novelist Winifred Holtby and fellow-feminist Vera Brittain, and along the street from the painter Augustus John. In the past, Thomas Carlyle, the Victorian sage, had lived hereabouts.

The play was clearly divided in two, so we shared out mornings and afternoons alternately. We had only four weeks to rehearse. The first week was spent normally, reading and partly-reading. Frank Finlay, playing the accused, was defending himself. The prosecuting counsel was Blair Booth (BB).

The second week, I noticed that BB was having a little trouble with the lines, and even referring to the script did not always help. Barristers are like actors in that they must carry in their heads the shape of their arguments. I thought I might recall classical Roman shrewdness of Cicero. Cicero tells us that a law case should be held in the mind like a house. The barrister enters and conducts his argument as he moves from room to room, using detail as the ornaments in the rooms remind him. So the case is assembled as the barrister completes his tour. Many think that this advice of Cicero's is the first literary mention of memory. I disagree. The Greeks thought of it, but they called it recollection. At all events, at the moment I thought I had better not mention Cicero. Sometimes BB would nearly get it right, then the effort would exhaust him and he would subside. Playing the judge, I was on the same level, close to him, and noted with some sympathy the perspiration that accompanied his efforts. I too began to perspire. In the middle of a cross-examination, he would suddenly stop, and his eyes would glass over as they peered inwardly. From my experience at Malvern, I could tell that the imagination was not involved, this was a straight tussle between the mind and the memory. He had lost sight of the dramatic situation. All that mattered to him was the right word.

I was reminded of the high wall at the Olympia Horse Show. The horse and rider approach, determined to conquer it; then suddenly, when about to take off, the horse shies away. The baulked rider withdraws, gathers the horse to its senses, then with clenched teeth advances again; and, just as it is about to rise, the horse remembers the previous attempt and shies away again. BB was like that. As the rehearsals progressed, the director and the cast showed much sympathy. This was made easy by the news at the end of the second week that Archer had won his real-life court case. Delight for Archer was mixed with a flickering doubt as to how the Press would now receive the play. I was glad that I had, earlier on, made up my mind about it. The situation was interesting.

The third week was much the same. The pauses were slimming down – but not enough. Actors who have done much television, like BB, get used to the one-line dialogue of the medium. The memory becomes rusty, uneasy when faced with the particularly formal dialogue of the court.

In the classical theatre, the actors understand the underlying grounds of the plays so well that it automatically develops and binds the performance. In the modern theatre, this abstraction which underpins the performance evolves through rehearsal. It is lived by the actors, and the audience unwittingly absorbs it. BB's uncertain breaks were disturbing this hidden growth, sometimes leading to paraphrasing the text which resulted in further confusion. In distress one day, I exploded in defence of the text. My colleagues looked at me silently, in some

164

embarrassment. I wished I had said nothing. I was too old for such capers. 'It will be all right on the night!' It would be a close thing.

The fourth week was disturbed; BB was rehearsing with the individual witnesses of the court scene. The second half of the play was displayed for the first time – to everyone's delight; full of energy and humour and the right words. Final fittings, then the cash handouts for subsistence and travel. All actors are now supposed to have cars. There are no company train calls, now. The theatre like everything else is dissolving into its parts. Archer saw a final run-through – he was very discreet. Much work would have to be done before we opened in London. Hollowly I reminded myself, that is what try-outs are for.

Travelling to Bath on Sunday, I was again buoyed up by the countryside, its beauty and care. Bath lies in a hollow, and this Sunday it was packed with tourists. I was living in the Westgate, and after depositing my chattels I drifted round the crowded streets. I find Bath curiously unfocused. Being in a hollow, everything is reversed. The interesting crescents are built on the hills, the Abbey is sunk into a trough of the town. And gulls everywhere, a suitable bird for the Roman remains. To me the Romans are the first mechanicals of Europe; I could find little to rejoice at in the propinquity of the Baths to the Abbey.

Other matters were absorbing my mind. Was anyone worrying about the play? Rejoicing in the coming into age of the individual, I should have rejoiced at the display of individuality shown by the company. Everywhere it was the same. It was not my business. Someone would do something.

There is always a fresh brush of optimism when a play moves from the rehearsal room into the theatre. A feeling that everything will come right, all ills will be dissolved in the capacious maw of the auditorium; what it always needed was an audience. And there is something about getting into a dressing room, putting on different clothes, listening to the noises, and the calls, examining the space. Indeed, now that we were acting in a replica of the Old Bailey, it seemed that the play might become coherent in all its parts. But that was only a first flush. As time passed, if old cracks were literally papered over in rewrites, new flaws mysteriously were revealed. It would have been less painful if BB was obnoxious, but he was a charming person and, as he assured me, he loved his garden.

There is always in every sphere a psychological moment for action. The theatre is no different. The time was long passed here when any action could have been taken – but as I reminded myself weakly, that was what try-outs were for. Was there time for BB to get hold of the part so that the court scene might have that seamless texture that was the director's and, it must be said, Archer's aim? Meanwhile the gulls of Bath were persecuting me. One night, they wakened me at three in the morning. Next day I changed my hotel.

Monday and Tuesday, we had the normal rehearsals. Our first night was Wednesday 19 August. A run-through in the afternoon, then the first night at 7.45 pm. I was relaxing in my dressing room as I normally do when Peter Gardner, our Manager, hurried into my room. 'Some idiot's left a bomb in the theatre, and we might have to get out,' and he left. I could not help smiling, for it was so characteristic of the Archer ambience as created by the Press. A few minutes later, Peter came back and said that the theatre was being evacuated, and I would have to get out. Apparently someone had phoned the box-office and said he'd left a bomb in the theatre, and it would go off in an hour's time. The box-office clerk didn't catch the name of the caller. It was all becoming bizarre.

I had seen judges walking fully dressed through the streets at the opening of Parliament, and I decided to wear my wig to meet the public. The apparition might bring some confidence. There was so much going on that, alas, it raised only a smile. After a few moments we were guided round the streets to an hotel to wait until the search was over. A large sedan-chair filled one corner of the foyer of the hotel, behind a large basket of flowers. I climbed over the flowers and waited, still and relaxed. Visitors to the hotel passed in front of me, nodding and smiling.

I had been sitting there for five minutes when our Clerk of the Court, Peter Clapham, wigless, came up to me, 'Have you heard? A man at Hungerford's gone mad, and he's shooting everything that moves in the village.' I stared at him. 'It's true,' he said, and hurried away. Hungerford is between London and Bath. No wonder the police had cleared the theatre, as terror spreads like lightning. Not everyone had heard, but people were moving about vaguely, clearly uncertain what was happening. In a few brief moments I had been given a devastating demonstration of the irrational and volatile nature of our society, clearly increased by the speed with which news of it gets around. The irrational had been around for a long time. They knew about it in fifth-century Athens. Greek tragedy had been the cybernetic response to it, the saying 'Nothing too much' was the guide for it. Until the twentieth century, the illusion persisted that man was a rational animal, but it was not so. As long as men regarded the individual as dispensable matter, the irrational would thrive. Only when each life was given value could humanity thrive.

There was a new dimension to our society. The volatile had always been there; until now, constrained by the heaviness of things. But with the discovery of unseen, weightless energies in the universe, each individual became vulnerable to self-destructive impulses that were immediate and involved first the destruction of others. Light, for all its benefits, had its dark side.

The curtain went up on the play an hour later. Such was the atmosphere surrounding it, the most that could be said was that it passed. Comments were uncertain. The reversal of the scenes caused a little confusion. Most people's lives are governed by the order of the alphabet. But what could not be denied was the energy brought to the piece, particularly by Frank Finlay. Energy is a great persuader in the theatre.

What was most evident was the public's desire to see the play. Not only was the theatre sold out but there were large queues for returns. Clearly Archer and his work commanded a large interest of the public. It was the first time in my life that I had met such a phenomenon. Before the war, C. B. Cochran's revues, when produced at Manchester prior to running at the London Pavilion, evoked a somewhat similar effusion of interest that was mostly professional; and at Stratford in 1950 there was almost hysteria approaching the last night. But this was something different. If it was a class thing (murmurs of 'bourgeois' could be picked up), then it was a very large class. Besides, Archer himself was highly professional. This was evident not only in the amused, knowing deference he accorded me as an old person, but in what I had seen of his flat. Unlike mine, created by my untidiness to Curigwen's lasting despair, Archer's flat is beautifully measured to satisfy the politician's desire for order and grace, and also, with its discreet layers of bound books surrounding the area for conversation, the artist's successful wooing of civilization. The elevation above the Houses of Parliament gave it an air of mysterious movement, relieved of earthly anchors. Clearly, a great deal of research went into Archer's life. But this was precisely what the new world demanded, though few knew how to go about it.

The cloud of unknowability that hung over Bath persisted until the weekend. I decided to return to London on the Sunday. There was little I could do about the piece. Decisions lay elsewhere. Archer's idea to have the chief law officer defending himself released us from the conventional playing of court scenes. Thus I felt I could play the Judge with a much greater intensity than is usual, and interest myself in the characters as though it was all taking place in a drawing room.

What was disturbing me was the fact, presented by this experience, that the notion of the individual which had grasped me years earlier when I first read Kierkegaard, and that had been made obligatory by the discoveries of science, was going sadly wrong. An election had just been fought in Britain and the party that stood for the individual, for freedom of choice, had triumphed. Again, while I found the Christian insight central to my understanding of myself, the Church was hopelessly doomed to a fruitless repetition. It was absurd. I was going through one of my periodic fits of depression when I couldn't do my sums. I was reaching out for Curigwen. Not that she could help me greatly; she had her own kind of despair. But to sit in company with someone who is dear to you in a silent colloquy seems to cream off the splurge and let the light in.

I returned to Bath on the Monday morning in time to attend a rehearsal call at the theatre – to be greeted with the news that BB had graciously resigned his part. It would be played that evening by his understudy, who had apparently been rehearsing intensely during the week, until a replacement arrived later. I did not enquire any further. I could not really express my gratitude to BB sufficiently. The pain that he had gone through during his period of rehearsal and playing had been wonderfully revealing – to me. Also, I could not help thinking how well the moves followed the Archer tradition of politics. No fuss; accomplished at a weekend, of course; a short-term and a long-term solution; and BB left to cultivate his garden.

What could I say to the journalist who phoned to ask about the trouble in the company? Trouble? The rehearsal period had been a trifle short, particularly when compared with the long days at the National. But trouble? No more than might be expected on a try-out. That, after all, is what try-outs are for.

The understudy was very good, and improved with every performance. He played out Bath, and the first half of the Manchester week until Jeffry Wickham took over for the rest of the tour and London. The reviews at Bath and Manchester were so confused, reflecting the highly ambivalent situation that existed between Archer and the Press, that I paid little attention to them then or later in London. My interest shifted to two things, Archer as a phenomenon in the theatre, and my own situation in this moment of time. During the week at Manchester I reflected on the first, mixed up with rehearsals for the replacement.

Since starting in the theatre back in 1929 in a somewhat overblown actor–manager's company, the structure of the theatre and how its organization responded to the changes in society had fascinated me. In the fifty years between 1930 and 1980, the changes that had occurred in the communication of art and information had been the most dramatic, universal and complex in the history of civilization, and I had kept time with them. From listening in the dark on a wireless crystal set to appearing before the latest television camera, from Shakespeare to Jeffrey Archer, from the proscenium arch to theatre-in-the-round. Usually, I analyse these matters under the rubrics of insight, technique and energy.

This time I felt I could drop the first two, insight and technique, and concentrate on what I thought was becoming the foremost concern not only in science, but in art, the nature of energy. At Edinburgh the Fringe had expanded as more young people realized that its mode of production suited their expense of energy. But the enterprise there was very low-key compared to the production I was now involved in. The difference between them was not in the quality of the imagination or the technical abilities of those employed, but purely financial. Money, its availability and disposal, had become central. Until the oil crisis in 1974, the theatre with the other arts had existed on a modest commercialism combined with a limited private patronage, all geared to the endurable costs of the time. Since 1974, costs in every direction had soared; money had increased but in the process become cheaper.

With peace, audiences were increasing as communications expanded, and diversity was apparent everywhere. The fundamental change that was overcoming society had been first seen by Newton, that the world was never at rest, everything moves. For almost three hundred years after Newton the world had adjusted itself to the heaviness of gravity, slowly moving away from the flat-earth assumptions of the classical world. Now, within a lifetime, not only was the world never at rest, but it was moving at relatively great speeds in response to powers that were weightless and invisible. Ideas were meaningless to cope with the fluctuations in this moving scene. The only thing that mattered was a display of energy that could be trusted.

At the end of the Manchester week, after this somewhat simplified analysis, I came to the conclusion that Archer's great appeal to the public lay in his energy. As stars in their rotation gather strength and light, so Archer became the focus for those agencies in our changing environment, financial, technical and otherwise, that thrive on the energies of such as Archer. Alas, there were not many about. If this was an insight, the example of Archer was a guide as to how the technique of the arts might move. The recognition of bundles of energy moving freely in the space of civilization. It was really absurd for me to go on like this. Everyone was satisfied with repetition. But there was always something happening to stimulate me to opposition.

At the end of the Manchester week, I came across a book by J. Z. Young, a distinguished physiologist, putting forward the proposition that the philosopher was the only person suitably placed to say some-thing about how the mind works. After my recent experience with BB, this was ludicrous. And yet it made me think whether any artist had the right to explore the means by which art is brought to the light. Trust the artist and his inspiration, no matter how it came. Art entertained. It was not to be taken seriously. This was the view pedalled in a society overtly dedicated to the enhancement of the individual. And not merely in Britain but everywhere, even as far as the Soviet Union, the category of the individual was beginning to alter the concept of politics and religion.

In the meantime, it gave me enormous pleasure to play the Judge in Archer's play with all the controlled energy I could muster.

Manchester audiences filled the enormous Palace Theatre for our week. We had only Brighton now before London. We had a new voice in the play, and the empty spaces were being filled in. Although Curigwen was away visiting, I decided to spend the Sunday at home before going on to Brighton on Monday morning. I had a chaste Sunday on sparse meals and thought.

As I was moving through our empty flat, the various strands of my life seemed to be converging on some sort of field of self-knowledge that was uniquely mine, because all the differences that potentially existed in my nature had settled into a kind of coherence imposed by me. Just as I had, in an elementary way, worked out the significance of Archer's energy in my area of work, so I now felt I must demonstrate myself as a model of individual sensibility. But I could not do this directly, as a politician or a preacher might. I could only do it in a way that left people free to reject it. I wanted no disciples. I had never belonged to any political party. My religious worship was usually governed by the beauty of the service rather than any truth I might receive.

The self of the primary artist, the creator, the dramatist, the composer, the painter is full of enough unconventional detail, as a rule, to throw light on his work, and interest on his life. But the secondary artist, the interpreter is regarded as an empty vessel to be filled by the object he is creating; and usually the secondary artist possesses those gifts, be he actor or musician, to satisfy these demands. I had now reached the situation, after my experiences of the last few years, to leap out of the straitjacket in which actors are usually imprisoned. My explorations had really begun with Kierkegaard's 'Subjectivity is reality, subjectivity is the truth.' This had meant moving from the objective world of description to the inward world of feeling, from the 'what' of things to the 'how' of things. But just as I had gone beyond Kierkegaard earlier on with the *The Infinite Guarantee*, so I now felt I must attempt to find something more precise than the inward world of feeling, of spirit. The spirit moves. It was really a quest for energy. If I have a desperate search in front of me, usually something turns up. I must put my hopes on Brighton.

Brighton was really my last opportunity to bring together what the irrational movements of the last few weeks meant to me. After the recent Archer case, once the play opened in London everything would be somewhat askew, taking some time to settle down.

At Malvern I had, after a lifetime of use, unified in a way my mind, memory and imagination. I could not have done this without the range of work I had done in the theatre, or the interests that had spawned into neighbouring disciplines like biology and physics. Evolution begins in simple movement and proceeds to complication. I have always stopped short before sinking in the complications. This movement is as true in the theatre as it is anywhere else. It was possible, I thought, to draw a kind of basic analogy between things that moved. But again, to stop short when they showed independent life.

The events at Bath punctuated by my colleague's struggles to bring his mind and memory into tandem convinced me that only art in all its diversity could be resorted to as a balm in the irrational and volatile world of today. Since we had come some way in recognizing the universality of the individual gene, it was time to start on the mind, which was also universal and unique, creating that beauty by which we live. The irony was that the artist could not do it on his own; he had to borrow from science, just as science had to use art.

The play opened to packed houses, which were to continue through the week. I was staying at the Sheraton on the front, as near to the sea as I could get. The hotel had an excellent restaurant. After breakfast every morning, I would cross over to the rails that look down on the beach and the sea, from which all life had spawned.

The weather was unpropitious almost the whole week. The wind and rain enveloped the front in visible swathes of mist that did much to protect my solitude. It was an ambience to concentrate the mind, and a place, looking over to Europe, to evoke memories. Beyond the grey sea, in the mists, was France. There in Paris, in the seventeenth century, Pascal, peering at the heavens, had confessed that the eternal silence of these infinite spaces terrified him. But if they were now silent, there was, thanks to Maxwell, a great potential for bearing sounds and

171

greetings. Maxwell had filled them with his equations. Again, Pascal's faith had been grounded on the Old Testament God of Abraham, Isaac and Jacob. Now there was no room for God in a space–time continuum. As Brecht saw, God had moved inward.

To my left, towards the East along the Channel, lay Dover Beach – where Matthew Arnold, brooding on faith a century ago, had heard its 'melancholy, long, withdrawing roar/Retreating, to the breath/Of the night-wind ...' I could not follow that.

I turned to my right, looking towards the West. Beyond the ocean lay America and the New World. That was how it appeared to those escaping from a tyrannous Europe. But it was no longer new, or could not appropriate an unusual degree of novelty. Heading for peace in our time, the whole world was waiting to experience a new birth.

Before turning away from the Atlantic, my mind settled on a small village in Cornwall, Poldhu. When forming the *Bedside Book*, I had had occasion to follow up the implications of Maxwell's discoveries – the reason being that he himself seemed to see so little future for them. But then scientists are the last people to recognize what is new in their discoveries. Rutherford, as we have seen, saw no future in his splitting of the atom. And Maxwell, faced with the sceptical, mechanistic views of his colleagues, underestimated the great originality of an insight that is one of the great turning points of science and, in my view, history – the propagation of electromagnetic radiation in the vacuum. Space was no longer empty.

It did not go unnoticed. Heinrich Hertz, a German scientist, with some elementary instruments created Maxwell's waves and the receivers to detect them, and he was able to confirm experimentally that the waves moved with the speed of light. Even scientists of the day could not accept the idea of a wave oscillating in nothing. It took the Italian entrepreneur Guglielmo Marconi to realize the great potential of Maxwell's fields. Obsessed by it, he carried out a number of experiments in Italy and England until eventually, to confound the mathematicians, he set up an experiment to test Maxwell's waves over the Atlantic, a great space of flat ocean.

Poldhu, in Cornwall, was the issuing point for the signal, a hut on the cliffs at St John's, Newfoundland, the point to receive it. The equipment was primitive, the belief in empty space complete. On 12 December 1901 at 12.30, a signal was sent out from Poldhu, and received at almost the same time in Newfoundland. Faintly but distinctly, Marconi heard the *pip-pip-pip* of the signal. He handed the phone to his assistant, Kemp. 'Can you hear anything?' he asked. Kemp listened. 'Yes,' he said, 'the letter S.'

I suddenly felt very foolish, and glad of the mist surrounding me. To Marconi, the great success of the experiment was the waves travelling a great distance in space unsupported by anything visible, and at a great speed. To me, as I remembered the experiment again, it was Kemp's reply, 'the letter S'. In the simplest way, he had shown a new movement of the mind, simultaneously to receive and transform.

Marconi's experiment initiated the great growth in the use of electromagnetic fields in radio, television, radar and most uses of energy in the modern world. Less evident has been its implication for the understanding of the mind, the memory and the imagination as experienced first by players, then everyone. Kemp's 'S' demonstrated the principle of simultaneity that exists between light, the mind, and the abstract field of Maxwell's equation in that they all exist in the present moment of time, the 'now' of the mind. Light is an electromagnetic phenomenon whose simplest access to the body is through the eye.

I suddenly felt very humble. Was I entitled to point out an omission in the thinking of a great scientist like Sherrington? Was he unaware of Maxwell and the fact that space was no longer empty? In his Gifford lectures, under the rubric 'The Wisdom of the Body', there is that piece of miraculous prose that describes the making of the eye. The qualities of the particular organs are elicited with the clinical accuracy of a great surgeon, but he does not notice that these beautifully evolved organs are surrounded by space. Nor does he look to space to provide that energy to the mind which at once separates the mind from the body yet keeps the mind within the shuffling of the earth. For it is the old earth that has provided the electricity and the magnetism that Maxwell saw were the same thing as light.

Under gravity, the body in all its parts can be measured, having form and weight. But not the mind, the memory or the imagination. These are invisible and weightless. If we want proof of these, we must turn to the artefacts of men. Above all, to the great art which through time men have created out of their imagination to stamp their lives with value and beauty.

I felt empty. I felt like mumbling all the plays I had ever been in, especially the great ones, as a sort of justification of my existence. But it would not do. If my life meant anything to me now, it was only as an individual. Only thus did I belong to the human race.

It was Sunday morning. The mists had lifted, the sea was calm. I turned towards the station to catch my train to London where I knew Curigwen would be waiting for me.

May 1988

Andrew died two weeks after the completion of
the final draft. He believed passionately in his
work and caught us all in his enthusiasm which
we believe infectious enough to extend to those
who did not have the great pleasure of knowing
him well and loving him dearly.

Curigwen, Marty, Harriet and John

Index